Patrice Espiche
The AI Formula for Employer Branding
Smart Tools Strong Brands

AF210528

The AI Formula for Employer Branding

Bibliografische Information der Deutschen Nationalbibliothek: Die Deutsche Nationalbibliothek verzeichnet diese Publikation in der Deutschen Nationalbibliografie; detaillierte bibliografische Daten sind im Internet über dnb.dnb.de abrufbar.

Die automatisierte Analyse des Werkes, um daraus Informationen insbesondere über Muster, Trends und Korrelationen gemäß §44b UrhG („Text und Data Mining") zu gewinnen, ist untersagt.

© 2025 Patrice Espiche

Verlag: BoD · Books on Demand GmbH, In de Tarpen 42, 22848 Norderstedt, bod@bod.de

Druck: Libri Plureos GmbH, Friedensallee 273, 22763 Hamburg

ISBN: 978-3-7597-6936-7

Table of Contents

Understanding Employer Branding in the Age of AI

Employer branding has undergone a remarkable evolution over the past few decades, transitioning from a largely transactional relationship between employers and employees to a rich, multifaceted dialogue that is increasingly influenced by external perceptions, digital platforms, and, most recently, artificial intelligence. Understanding this evolution is essential for organizations aiming to attract and retain top talent in today's competitive landscape.

Historically, employer branding emerged as a way for organizations to differentiate themselves in a crowded market. In the early days, the focus was primarily on creating an appealing workplace culture and benefits package, often communicated through traditional marketing channels. However, as the job market became more competitive and candidates gained greater access to information about potential employers, the concept of employer branding began to shift. No longer could organizations simply rely on their reputation or a few catchy slogans; they had to actively manage their brand in a way that resonated with both current and potential employees.

The rise of social media marked a significant turning point in the evolution of employer branding. Platforms such as LinkedIn, Glassdoor, and Twitter democratized information, allowing candidates to share their experiences and opinions about employers openly. This transparency shifted the power dynamics, placing more emphasis on employee advocacy and authentic representation of workplace culture. Companies were no longer just brands; they became subjects of review and discussion, with their reputations resting in the hands of their employees and the public.

As organizations began to recognize the importance of managing their employer brand actively, they started investing in initiatives aimed at enhancing employee engagement and satisfaction. The concept of the Employee Value Proposition (EVP) emerged as a strategic framework to articulate what employees can expect from their employer in exchange for their skills, experience, and commitment. The EVP became a cornerstone of employer branding strategies, guiding companies in crafting messages that aligned with their values and culture while appealing to the aspirations of their target talent pool.

In this context, the integration of technology into employer branding practices began to take shape. The advent of recruitment marketing software and applicant tracking systems (ATS) allowed organizations to streamline hiring processes and enhance candidate experiences. Job postings became more sophisticated, employing data analytics to target specific demographics and optimize ad placements. However, even with these advancements, employer branding often remained a function largely driven by human intuition and traditional marketing principles.

The introduction of artificial intelligence into the employer branding landscape marks the latest phase in this ongoing evolution. AI technologies are fundamentally reshaping the way organizations approach recruitment, engagement, and brand perception. With the ability to process vast amounts of data at unprecedented speeds, AI offers insights that can inform decision-making and strategy.

For instance, predictive analytics can help identify the characteristics of successful employees, guiding recruitment efforts toward candidates who are more likely to thrive within the organizational culture.
Moreover, AI-powered tools enable companies to deliver personalized experiences to candidates, effectively transforming the recruitment process into a more engaging and tailored journey. Chatbots, for example, can provide instant responses to candidate inquiries, ensuring that communication is seamless and efficient. This technology not only enhances the candidate experience but also alleviates the administrative burden on HR teams, allowing them to focus on more strategic initiatives.

However, the integration of AI into employer branding is not without its challenges. As organizations increasingly rely on algorithms and data-driven insights, they must be vigilant about potential pitfalls, including issues related to bias and fairness. AI systems are only as good as the data they are trained on, and if historical hiring practices have favored certain demographics over others, the algorithms may perpetuate these biases. Consequently, organizations must approach AI implementation with a commitment to ethical standards and transparency, ensuring that their AI solutions support inclusive hiring practices rather than hinder them.

In addition to these challenges, the rapid evolution of technology poses an ongoing dilemma for organizations striving to maintain an authentic and human-centric employer brand. As companies embrace AI tools to enhance their recruitment strategies, they must also remain mindful of the importance of personal connections and genuine interactions.

While AI can streamline processes and provide valuable insights, it cannot replace the intrinsic value of human relationships in the workplace. Therefore, a balance must be struck between leveraging technology and preserving the human touch that is essential to effective employer branding.

As we navigate the complexities of employer branding in the age of AI, it is crucial to recognize that this evolution is not a linear progression but rather a dynamic interplay of factors that continuously shape the employer-employee relationship. The rise of AI represents a significant opportunity for organizations to enhance their employer branding strategies, providing them with the tools to attract, engage, and retain talent in a way that aligns with the expectations of today's workforce.

This ongoing evolution calls for a new framework—one that encapsulates the multifaceted nature of employer branding in the AI era. The AI Prism framework, introduced in the following chapter, will serve as a guiding structure for how organizations can harness AI in a manner that aligns with their branding goals, ensuring their strategies are not only effective but also reflective of the values and culture they wish to communicate to both internal and external audiences.

Ultimately, the evolution of employer branding in the age of AI is a testament to the shifting landscape of talent acquisition and engagement. Organizations that embrace this change and leverage AI's capabilities will be well-positioned to build strong, authentic employer brands that resonate with potential and existing employees alike, fostering a workplace culture that is both inclusive and dynamic in the face of an ever-evolving job market.

Artificial intelligence is reshaping the landscape of recruitment, offering organizations unprecedented opportunities to enhance their hiring processes and strengthen their employer branding. In the modern recruitment era, AI acts as a catalyst, optimizing the way businesses connect with potential candidates and manage their talent pools. By automating routine tasks and providing data-driven insights, AI empowers HR professionals to focus on strategic initiatives that foster a compelling employer brand.

At the heart of AI's impact on recruitment lies its ability to analyze vast amounts of data quickly and accurately. Traditional recruitment methods often rely on subjective judgments and manual processes, which can be time-consuming and prone to bias. In contrast, AI algorithms can evaluate resumes, track candidate interactions, and assess various applicant metrics in real time. This enables organizations to streamline their recruitment processes significantly. For instance, AI-powered applicant tracking systems can sift through hundreds, if not thousands, of applications in minutes, allowing recruiters to identify the most qualified candidates based on predetermined criteria. This efficiency not only saves valuable time but also ensures that hiring decisions are grounded in objective data rather than gut feelings.

Moreover, AI enhances the recruitment experience for candidates. Chatbots and virtual assistants, powered by natural language processing, can engage with applicants in real time, answering their queries and guiding them through the application process. This immediate support can alleviate candidate anxiety and create a more positive experience, reflecting well on the organization's employer brand. Furthermore, these AI-driven tools can be programmed to provide personalized feedback to candidates, regardless of whether they are successful in securing a position. This level of engagement fosters a sense of respect and transparency, which is increasingly important to job seekers today.

AI also plays a pivotal role in enhancing diversity and inclusion within recruitment strategies. Traditional hiring processes can inadvertently perpetuate biases, leading to homogeneous workforces that lack diverse perspectives. AI can help mitigate these issues by anonymizing resumes and removing identifying information that may lead to bias—such as names, genders, or educational backgrounds—from the initial screening process. Additionally, AI tools can analyze job descriptions for biased language that may deter underrepresented groups from applying. By focusing on skills and competencies rather than demographic factors, organizations can create a more inclusive hiring process that attracts a wider array of talent. This commitment to diversity not only enriches the workplace but also strengthens the organization's employer brand among candidates who prioritize inclusivity.

Another significant advantage of AI in recruitment is the ability to leverage predictive analytics. By analyzing historical data and trends, organizations can make informed predictions about future hiring needs and candidate success. For example, AI can identify which recruitment channels yield the highest-quality candidates or which attributes correlate most strongly with long-term employee retention. This capability enables HR teams to allocate resources more effectively and tailor their recruitment strategies to align with organizational goals. Predictive analytics also allows organizations to proactively address potential talent shortages by identifying skill gaps within their workforce and developing targeted recruitment campaigns to fill those gaps.

Personalization is another area where AI excels, enabling organizations to create tailored marketing campaigns that resonate with potential candidates. AI-driven tools can analyze candidate behavior and preferences to craft personalized outreach strategies. For instance, machine learning algorithms can segment candidates based on their interests, qualifications, and past interactions with the brand, allowing recruiters to send targeted job alerts and content that speaks directly to each candidate's aspirations. This level of personalization not only enhances the candidate experience but also reinforces the employer brand as one that understands and values individual preferences.

In addition to improving the recruitment process, AI provides organizations with the ability to continuously refine their strategies through robust analytics and reporting. By collecting and analyzing data at every stage of the recruitment funnel, HR professionals can gain valuable insights into the effectiveness of their efforts. For example, metrics such as time-to-hire, candidate satisfaction scores, and offer acceptance rates can be monitored in real time, allowing organizations to identify bottlenecks and make data-driven adjustments. This commitment to continuous improvement not only enhances the recruitment process but also signals to candidates that the organization values innovation and responsiveness—a key aspect of a strong employer brand.

Despite these advantages, the implementation of AI in recruitment is not without challenges. Organizations must remain vigilant about the ethical considerations surrounding data privacy and bias. As AI systems are trained on historical data, there is a risk that they may inadvertently replicate existing biases present in that data. Therefore, it is crucial for organizations to regularly audit their AI systems and ensure that they are promoting fairness and inclusivity.

Transparent communication about how AI is being used in the recruitment process can also help build trust among candidates, assuring them that their data is being handled responsibly.

Furthermore, as AI becomes more integrated into recruitment strategies, HR professionals must be equipped with the skills to leverage these technologies effectively. This may involve upskilling existing teams or collaborating with AI specialists to ensure that recruitment strategies are aligned with best practices. By fostering a culture of learning and adaptability, organizations can position themselves to successfully navigate the evolving landscape of AI-driven recruitment.

In this age of rapid technological advancement, the role of AI in modern recruitment is becoming increasingly integral to building a strong employer brand. By harnessing AI's capabilities, organizations can enhance their recruitment processes, create engaging candidate experiences, and foster inclusive hiring practices. As the talent landscape continues to evolve, those organizations that embrace AI as a strategic partner in their recruitment efforts will not only attract top talent but also cultivate an authentic employer brand that resonates with both potential and existing employees. Thus, the power of AI in recruitment is not just about efficiency; it is about redefining what it means to be an employer of choice in a competitive marketplace.

The rise of artificial intelligence (AI) presents both significant challenges and remarkable opportunities for organizations navigating the complex landscape of employer branding. As companies strive to position themselves as attractive employers, they must adapt to the swift changes driven by AI technologies.

This adaptation requires a nuanced understanding of the challenges that may impede progress, alongside a recognition of the opportunities that AI can unlock.

One of the most pressing challenges in the AI era is the potential for increased competition in talent acquisition. As more organizations adopt AI-driven recruitment tools, the market becomes saturated with companies vying for the same pool of candidates. This heightened competition can dilute the effectiveness of traditional employer branding strategies. Employers may find it increasingly difficult to differentiate themselves in a crowded marketplace where AI is used to showcase job openings, streamline applications, and enhance candidate experiences.

Organizations must therefore invest in innovative branding strategies that leverage AI to create unique narratives and experiences that resonate with prospective employees.

Another challenge lies in the quality and integrity of data utilized by AI systems. AI algorithms depend on large datasets to learn and make decisions, but if the underlying data is flawed, biased, or incomplete, the outcomes can be detrimental. For instance, an AI tool trained on a dataset lacking diversity may inadvertently perpetuate existing biases in recruitment, leading to a homogeneous workforce that fails to reflect the broader society. This not only undermines efforts toward inclusivity but can also damage an organization's reputation as an employer that values diversity. Companies need to prioritize the ethical sourcing of data and implement rigorous auditing processes to ensure that their AI tools are based on comprehensive and representative datasets.

Furthermore, the integration of AI into employer branding strategies can create a disconnect between candidates and the human aspect of recruitment. While AI can analyze resumes and predict candidate suitability with remarkable accuracy, over-reliance on algorithms may lead to impersonal interactions that alienate applicants. Candidates often seek authentic connections and personalized experiences during the hiring process. Organizations must strike a balance between leveraging AI capabilities to enhance efficiency and maintaining a human-centric approach that fosters genuine engagement.

Employers should consider using AI to augment rather than replace human interaction, ensuring that candidates feel valued and heard throughout their journey.

In addition to these challenges, organizations face the imperative of aligning their AI initiatives with broader employer branding goals. The use of AI should not be an isolated endeavor; it must be integrated into a comprehensive branding strategy that reflects the organization's values and mission. For instance, an organization that prides itself on innovation must ensure that its AI tools are not only cutting-edge but also aligned with its commitment to fostering creativity and collaboration among employees. This alignment requires a clear roadmap that connects AI initiatives to the overarching narrative of the employer brand, ensuring consistency across all touchpoints in the candidate experience.

Despite these challenges, the opportunities presented by AI for employer branding are profound. One of the most significant advantages is the power of predictive analytics. Organizations can harness AI to analyze historical hiring data, employee performance metrics, and market trends to forecast future talent needs and identify ideal candidates. This capability allows companies to adopt a proactive approach to recruitment, streamlining their efforts and ensuring that they are targeting the right talent at the right time.

By leveraging predictive analytics, organizations can enhance their employer branding by showcasing their commitment to strategic foresight and effective workforce planning.

AI also enables highly personalized job marketing campaigns that cater to the unique preferences and aspirations of potential candidates. Through machine learning algorithms, organizations can analyze user behavior on job portals and social media platforms to deliver tailored content and job recommendations. This level of personalization not only enhances the candidate experience but also strengthens the employer brand by demonstrating an understanding of individual needs and preferences. Candidates are more likely to engage with an employer that takes the time to understand their career ambitions and aligns opportunities accordingly.

Moreover, AI can significantly improve the recruitment process by automating repetitive tasks, such as resume screening and interview scheduling. This automation frees up valuable time for HR professionals to focus on higher-level strategic initiatives, such as building relationships with candidates and fostering a positive employer brand. By streamlining these processes, organizations can enhance their responsiveness to candidates, creating a more engaging experience that reflects positively on their brand.

The integration of AI into employer branding also opens avenues for enhanced employee engagement and retention. AI-driven tools can facilitate continuous feedback loops, allowing employees to share their insights and experiences in real time. This feedback can be invaluable in shaping an organization's culture and branding efforts, as it provides direct insight into employee perceptions and satisfaction levels. Companies that prioritize employee voice and actively respond to feedback are likely to cultivate a strong employer brand that resonates with both existing and prospective employees.

Lastly, the global nature of the modern workforce presents an opportunity for organizations to leverage AI in adapting their employer branding strategies to diverse cultural contexts. AI tools can analyze regional trends, preferences, and values, enabling organizations to tailor their branding efforts to resonate with specific markets. This cultural sensitivity not only enhances the effectiveness of recruitment campaigns but also positions the organization as a global employer that values diversity and inclusion across borders.

In conclusion, while the challenges posed by AI in the realm of employer branding are significant, they are not insurmountable. Organizations that embrace the transformative potential of AI—while remaining vigilant about ethical considerations, data integrity, and the human element of recruitment—will find themselves well positioned to thrive in the competitive talent landscape.

By turning challenges into opportunities, businesses can develop authentic employer brands that resonate deeply with candidates and employees alike, ultimately leading to sustained success in attracting and retaining top talent.

Introducing the AI Prism Framework for Employer Branding

In the rapidly evolving landscape of employer branding, organizations face the challenge of differentiating themselves in a crowded market. As businesses strive to attract and retain top talent, they often find themselves at a crossroads where traditional branding strategies may fall short. Enter the AI Prism Framework, a novel approach designed to harness the power of artificial intelligence in developing a compelling employer brand that resonates with both potential and existing employees.

The AI Prism Framework is built on the premise that effective employer branding is multidimensional, requiring a comprehensive understanding of how various AI tools and strategies can be interwoven to create a cohesive narrative. This framework provides a structured method for organizations to align their branding efforts with the capabilities of AI, maximizing their reach and impact. By viewing employer branding through the prism of AI, companies can dissect and analyze their strategies to ensure they are engaging, authentic, and sustainable.

At its core, the AI Prism Framework consists of four key components: Data, Insights, Engagement, and Adaptation. Each of these elements plays a distinct role in enhancing employer branding efforts and serves as a critical lens through which organizations can evaluate their current practices and future initiatives.

Data is the foundational element of the AI Prism. In the age of AI, data is abundant, but its value lies in how effectively it is collected, analyzed, and utilized.

Organizations must leverage data from various sources, such as employee feedback, recruitment metrics, and market trends, to gain a holistic view of their employer brand. This data-driven approach enables companies to identify strengths and weaknesses in their branding strategies, ensuring that they are grounded in reality rather than assumptions. Moreover, AI tools can automate data collection and analysis, allowing HR professionals to focus on strategic decision-making rather than being bogged down by manual processes.

Insights, the second component of the AI Prism, refers to the actionable intelligence derived from data analysis. AI algorithms can sift through vast amounts of information to uncover patterns and trends that may not be immediately apparent. For example, sentiment analysis can provide organizations with a clearer understanding of how their employer brand is perceived in the market. This insight can inform the development of targeted messaging and campaigns that resonate with specific demographics. Furthermore, insights can facilitate predictive analytics, allowing organizations to anticipate talent needs and adjust their branding strategies accordingly.

Engagement is the third dimension of the AI Prism, focusing on how organizations interact with both potential and current employees. AI-powered tools can enhance engagement through personalized communication, tailored experiences, and interactive platforms. For instance, chatbots can provide immediate responses to candidate queries, creating a more responsive and engaging recruitment process. Additionally, AI-driven content personalization can ensure that job seekers receive relevant information that speaks to their interests and aspirations, thereby fostering a deeper connection with the brand. By prioritizing engagement, organizations can create an inclusive environment that values the voices and perspectives of all employees.

Adaptation, the final component of the AI Prism, emphasizes the importance of agility in employer branding. The job market is continually changing, influenced by economic conditions, technological advancements, and shifting employee expectations. Organizations must be prepared to pivot their branding strategies in response to these dynamics. AI can play a crucial role in this regard by providing real-time analytics and monitoring brand perception across various channels. This enables HR leaders to respond swiftly to emerging trends and adapt their messaging accordingly, ensuring that the employer brand remains relevant and appealing.

A critical aspect of the AI Prism Framework is the interplay between its components. Data informs insights, which in turn drive engagement, while engagement provides feedback that can lead to further data collection and analysis. This cyclical relationship creates a feedback loop that reinforces the employer brand, making it more resilient and adaptable to change.

Implementation of the AI Prism Framework requires a strategic approach. Organizations must first assess their current employer branding efforts and identify gaps in their use of AI. This might involve conducting a thorough audit of existing data sources, evaluating the effectiveness of current engagement strategies, and determining how agile the organization is in adapting to market changes. Once gaps have been identified, companies can begin to integrate AI tools into their branding strategies, ensuring that each component of the AI Prism is addressed.

Furthermore, it is essential for organizations to foster a culture of innovation and learning, empowering HR teams to experiment with new AI technologies and methodologies. This might include investing in training programs that enhance digital literacy and data analytics capabilities within HR departments. By equipping teams with the skills necessary to harness AI effectively, organizations can cultivate a proactive approach to employer branding that embraces change rather than fearing it.

Finally, as businesses embark on their journey with the AI Prism Framework, it is crucial to maintain a focus on the human element of employer branding. While AI tools offer significant advantages in data processing and analysis, the heart of employer branding lies in authentic connections with employees and candidates. Organizations should strive to balance the technological aspects of their branding strategies with genuine human interactions, ensuring that their employer brand reflects the values and culture that make them unique.

In conclusion, the AI Prism Framework provides a robust and innovative approach to employer branding in the age of artificial intelligence. By leveraging the interconnected components of data, insights, engagement, and adaptation, organizations can create a dynamic and compelling employer brand that attracts and retains top talent. As the workforce continues to evolve, businesses that embrace the AI Prism Framework will not only enhance their branding efforts but will also position themselves as leaders in the competitive talent landscape.

In the rapidly evolving landscape of employer branding, companies are increasingly recognizing the need to align their artificial intelligence (AI) strategies with overarching brand goals.

This alignment is crucial not only for attracting top talent but also for cultivating an authentic brand narrative that resonates with both potential and existing employees. To effectively harness AI in employer branding, organizations must first identify their unique brand identity, values, and mission, and then map these elements to AI-driven initiatives that enhance visibility, engagement, and personalization.

A foundational step in this alignment process is understanding the core objectives of employer branding. Companies need to articulate what differentiates them in the marketplace, focusing on aspects such as company culture, employee value proposition, and career development opportunities. Once these elements are clearly defined, businesses can explore how AI can amplify and express these brand attributes in a compelling manner.

For instance, predictive analytics can play a pivotal role in identifying the traits and characteristics of successful employees within an organization. By analyzing historical data on employee performance, retention rates, and engagement levels, AI algorithms can help HR professionals pinpoint the qualities that align with the company's brand values. Armed with these insights, organizations can refine their recruitment strategies to attract candidates who not only possess the right skills but also fit well within the company culture. This data-driven approach ensures that the organization's branding efforts are both targeted and effective, enhancing the overall quality of hires while simultaneously reinforcing the brand's identity.

Moreover, personalizing the candidate experience is fundamental to aligning AI strategies with employer branding goals. AI-powered tools enable companies to tailor their communication and engagement efforts based on individual profiles and preferences. For instance, chatbots can facilitate real-time interactions with potential candidates, providing them with relevant information about the company and its culture. By delivering a customized experience, organizations can create a strong first impression that reflects their commitment to transparency and engagement—key components of an authentic employer brand.

Another critical aspect of aligning AI strategies with employer branding is leveraging social listening tools. Monitoring online conversations and sentiments about the brand can provide invaluable insights into how the organization is perceived in the job market. AI can analyze vast amounts of social media data, identifying trends and sentiments that inform branding strategies. By understanding public perception, companies can adjust their messaging and outreach efforts to better align with the expectations and values of their target audience. This proactive approach not only enhances the credibility of the employer brand but also demonstrates a willingness to listen and adapt, qualities that are increasingly valued by job seekers.

Furthermore, organizations should consider how AI can support inclusivity and diversity within their branding efforts. AI algorithms can help identify and eliminate biases in job descriptions, recruitment processes, and promotional materials. By ensuring that the language used in job postings is inclusive and appealing to a diverse audience, companies can position themselves as employers of choice for underrepresented groups.

This commitment to diversity not only enhances brand perception but also contributes to a richer workplace culture that fosters innovation and creativity. As organizations develop their AI strategies, it is also essential to establish clear metrics to evaluate the effectiveness of these initiatives.

This involves defining key performance indicators (KPIs) that align with branding goals, such as brand awareness, candidate engagement rates, and employee retention figures. By applying AI analytics, companies can track these metrics in real-time, adjusting their strategies as needed to ensure alignment with their branding objectives. This iterative approach to measurement fosters a culture of continuous improvement, allowing organizations to adapt to changing market conditions and evolving candidate expectations.

In addition, fostering cross-departmental collaboration is vital for aligning AI strategies with employer branding goals. HR, marketing, and IT teams must work together to create a cohesive brand narrative that is consistently communicated across all touchpoints. This collaboration can help ensure that AI tools are utilized effectively, with insights from various departments contributing to a holistic understanding of the employer brand. For example, marketing insights can inform HR about the types of content that resonate with target candidates, while HR data can guide marketing in crafting compelling messaging that reflects the company's values.

Another avenue for alignment is through the integration of AI into employee development programs. By utilizing AI-driven learning and development platforms, organizations can create personalized career paths for employees that align with their individual aspirations and the company's strategic goals. This not only enhances employee satisfaction and engagement but also reinforces the employer brand as a place that values growth and development. When employees see that their organization is invested in their futures, they are more likely to become brand ambassadors, sharing their positive experiences with potential candidates.

As businesses continue to navigate the complexities of the modern job market, aligning AI strategies with employer branding goals will be critical for long-term success. The integration of AI into recruitment, engagement, and retention efforts can create a more dynamic and responsive employer brand that resonates with a diverse workforce. By embracing data-driven insights, personalizing candidate experiences, and fostering an inclusive culture, organizations can position themselves as leaders in the talent marketplace.

Ultimately, the successful alignment of AI strategies with employer branding goals requires a commitment to authenticity and transparency. As companies leverage advanced technologies, they must remain mindful of the human element that underpins employer branding. By prioritizing genuine connections with employees and candidates alike, organizations can create a brand narrative that is not only compelling but also reflective of their true values and mission. In doing so, they will be well-equipped to attract and retain top talent in an increasingly competitive landscape, all while building a strong, authentic employer brand that stands the test of time.

The AI Prism Framework serves as a guiding beacon for organizations aiming to enhance their employer branding efforts through the strategic application of artificial intelligence. Comprising five key components—Data Intelligence, Personalization, Engagement, Authenticity, and Continuous Improvement—this framework illuminates how AI can be harnessed to create a compelling and authentic employer brand that resonates with both potential and existing employees.

Data Intelligence forms the foundation of the AI Prism. In the realm of employer branding, data is an invaluable asset that provides insights into candidate preferences, market trends, and organizational performance. By leveraging advanced analytics and machine learning algorithms, organizations can sift through vast amounts of data to identify patterns and predict future outcomes. This means going beyond basic metrics such as recruitment time and cost per hire. Instead, organizations can analyze candidate behaviors, engagement levels, and even sentiment analysis from social media and online reviews to understand what attracts top talent.

For instance, a company looking to improve its employer brand might employ AI-driven tools to analyze employee feedback and reviews across platforms like Glassdoor or LinkedIn. By identifying recurring themes—be it leadership effectiveness, workplace culture, or opportunities for growth—HR professionals can pinpoint strengths to highlight in their employer branding efforts and address weaknesses that may deter potential candidates. By grounding employer branding strategies in data intelligence, organizations ensure that their initiatives resonate with the realities of the job market and the specific needs of their target audience.

The second component of the AI Prism is Personalization. In a world where candidates are inundated with job offers and information, a one-size-fits-all approach to recruitment is no longer effective. AI enables organizations to deliver tailored experiences that cater to individual preferences and career aspirations. By utilizing AI algorithms, companies can create personalized content and job recommendations that resonate more deeply with candidates. For example, AI can analyze a candidate's past job applications, online behavior, and social media interactions to present them with opportunities that align with their skills and interests.

Moreover, personalization extends to communication. AI chatbots and virtual assistants can provide candidates with real-time answers to their inquiries, offer personalized guidance throughout the application process, and follow up with tailored messages based on the candidate's engagement history.

This level of personalization not only enhances the candidate experience but also fosters a sense of value and recognition, reinforcing the employer brand's commitment to its potential hires.

Engagement is the third key component of the AI Prism. Effective employer branding hinges on the ability to engage candidates and employees meaningfully. AI tools can facilitate this engagement through a variety of channels. For instance, AI-driven recruitment platforms can automate outreach and follow-ups, ensuring that candidates remain informed and engaged throughout the hiring process. Additionally, gamification elements powered by AI can be integrated into recruitment campaigns, making the experience more interactive and enjoyable for candidates. Such strategies not only attract candidates but also reflect an organization's innovative spirit, enhancing its employer brand.

Furthermore, engagement does not end with the recruitment process. AI can be employed to maintain ongoing communication and connection with employees, creating a sense of community and belonging. Regularly scheduled check-ins through AI tools can provide employees with opportunities to voice their opinions, share feedback, and engage with their peers, all of which contribute to a positive organizational culture and a strong employer brand.

Authenticity emerges as the fourth component of the AI Prism. In an era where candidates prioritize transparency and genuine connections with employers, organizations must leverage AI to present an authentic image of their culture and values. Data-driven storytelling, powered by AI, allows companies to craft compelling narratives that reflect the true employee experience. This can be achieved by utilizing AI to analyze employee-generated content, such as testimonials, blogs, and social media posts, to extract authentic stories that illuminate the organization's unique culture.

Moreover, AI can assist in measuring brand perception by analyzing sentiment across various digital channels. This provides organizations with real-time insights into how their employer brand is viewed by both current employees and potential candidates. By understanding these perceptions, companies can make informed adjustments to their branding strategies, ensuring that they remain authentic and aligned with their core values.

The final component of the AI Prism is Continuous Improvement. The dynamic nature of the labor market necessitates that organizations remain agile and responsive to changing trends and candidate expectations. Through AI-powered metrics and analytics, companies can continuously monitor the effectiveness of their employer branding strategies. This involves tracking key performance indicators (KPIs) such as candidate engagement rates, employee retention, and overall satisfaction levels.

By establishing a feedback loop that incorporates data analytics, organizations can identify areas for improvement and adapt their strategies accordingly. For example, if data reveals a high drop-off rate during the application process, HR teams can delve into the specifics to understand the underlying causes—be it a cumbersome application form or a lack of communication. This iterative approach fosters a culture of continuous improvement, ensuring that employer branding efforts evolve alongside the needs and preferences of the workforce.

In summary, the AI Prism Framework for employer branding offers a comprehensive approach that equips organizations with the tools and insights necessary to build a strong and authentic employer brand. By focusing on Data Intelligence, Personalization, Engagement, Authenticity, and Continuous Improvement, companies can leverage AI not only to attract top talent but also to create a meaningful and lasting connection with their workforce. As the job market evolves and candidates become increasingly discerning in their choices, the AI Prism stands as a vital resource for those seeking to thrive in an ever-changing landscape.

Attracting Talent: AI-Driven Recruitment Strategies

In the competitive landscape of talent acquisition, organizations are increasingly turning to predictive analytics to enhance their recruitment strategies. This powerful tool leverages historical data and advanced algorithms to forecast future hiring needs, candidate success, and overall workforce trends. By integrating predictive analytics into their recruitment processes, companies can make data-driven decisions that not only streamline their hiring efforts but also improve the quality of candidates they attract.

At its core, predictive analytics in recruitment involves analyzing patterns from various data sources—such as past hiring decisions, employee performance metrics, and market trends—to anticipate which candidates are most likely to succeed in specific roles. This is particularly vital in a time where organizations face a scarcity of top talent, and the cost of a bad hire can be substantial, both financially and culturally. By employing predictive analytics, HR professionals can mitigate these risks and strategically position their employer brand to attract the right talent.

One of the primary benefits of utilizing predictive analytics is its capability to enhance job descriptions and requirements. Traditional job postings often rely on generic criteria that may not accurately reflect the essential skills or attributes needed for success in a given role. With predictive analytics, organizations can analyze data from high-performing employees in similar positions to identify the key competencies that correlate with success. This refined approach allows companies to craft targeted job descriptions that resonate with ideal candidates, thereby drawing in applicants who are genuinely suited for the role.

Moreover, predictive analytics can assist in streamlining the sourcing process. By examining historical hiring data, organizations can determine which sourcing channels yield the highest quality candidates. For instance, if data reveals that candidates coming from specific universities tend to perform better within the organization, recruiters can prioritize those institutions in their outreach efforts. Similarly, analyzing social media engagement patterns can inform recruiters about where to focus their marketing efforts to reach potential candidates effectively. This strategic alignment not only enhances efficiency but also strengthens the employer brand by showcasing a commitment to finding the right cultural fit.

Another key aspect of predictive analytics is its ability to assess candidate suitability through advanced assessment tools. Traditional recruitment methods often rely on subjective evaluations of resumes and interviews, which can lead to biases and inconsistencies. In contrast, organizations utilizing predictive analytics can implement structured assessments that measure candidates' skills, cognitive abilities, and cultural fit against established benchmarks derived from successful incumbents. By leveraging data-driven assessments, companies can enhance the objectivity of their hiring processes while simultaneously reducing unconscious biases that may deter diverse talent.

Furthermore, predictive analytics can enhance the candidate experience by personalizing interactions throughout the recruitment journey. By analyzing candidate data, organizations can tailor communication and engagement efforts to meet individual needs. For example, if a candidate's application history shows an interest in professional development opportunities, recruiters can highlight training programs or mentorship initiatives during the interview process. This level of personalization not only improves the candidate experience but also reinforces the employer brand as one that values growth and development, making it more attractive to potential hires.

The application of predictive analytics extends beyond initial candidate assessments; it also plays a vital role in retention strategies. By analyzing employee turnover data, organizations can identify trends and predictors of attrition, such as job satisfaction scores, engagement levels, and external economic factors. Armed with these insights, HR leaders can proactively address retention challenges by implementing targeted strategies aimed at enhancing employee satisfaction and engagement.

For instance, if data suggests that employees in specific departments report lower satisfaction rates, organizations can investigate and address the underlying issues, demonstrating a commitment to employee well-being and fostering a strong employer brand.

Moreover, predictive analytics can facilitate strategic workforce planning. By examining data on hiring trends, workforce demographics, and market conditions, organizations can develop a forward-looking approach to talent acquisition. This enables them to anticipate future hiring needs and align their recruitment efforts with long-term business goals. Such strategic foresight not only positions organizations to attract top talent but also enhances their employer brand by portraying a clear vision for the future.

Implementing predictive analytics in recruitment, however, requires a thoughtful approach. Organizations must first invest in robust data collection and management systems to ensure the accuracy and validity of their insights. This includes gathering data from multiple sources, such as applicant tracking systems, employee surveys, and industry benchmarks. Additionally, HR professionals should be trained in data analysis techniques to effectively interpret and leverage predictive insights.

Ethical considerations also play a critical role in the deployment of predictive analytics. Organizations must ensure that their analytics practices are transparent and equitable, avoiding bias in algorithms that could disproportionately affect certain groups of candidates. By being proactive in addressing these ethical concerns, companies can build trust with candidates and reinforce their commitment to diversity and inclusion.

As organizations continue to navigate the complexities of talent acquisition, predictive analytics offers a powerful solution for enhancing recruitment strategies. By harnessing the potential of data-driven insights, organizations can attract top talent, streamline their hiring processes, and strengthen their employer brand. In an era where the competition for skilled professionals is fierce, those who effectively leverage predictive analytics will not only gain a competitive edge but also cultivate a reputation as a forward-thinking employer that prioritizes the success of its workforce.

Ultimately, the integration of predictive analytics into recruitment strategies represents a significant evolution in the way organizations approach talent acquisition. By embracing this innovative approach, companies can create a more informed, efficient, and human-centric recruitment process that resonates with both potential and existing employees. In a world where authenticity and alignment with organizational values are paramount, the use of predictive analytics can help organizations build a compelling employer brand that attracts and retains the best talent available.

In the fast-paced, competitive landscape of talent acquisition, crafting personalized job marketing campaigns has emerged as a vital strategy for organizations aiming to attract top candidates. Traditional one-size-fits-all approaches to recruitment marketing often miss the mark, leading to disengagement and a lack of authentic connections with potential applicants. By leveraging artificial intelligence, organizations can now create tailored, data-driven campaigns that resonate deeply with target audiences, enhancing both engagement and conversion rates.

At the core of personalized job marketing lies the ability to analyze vast amounts of data to understand candidate behavior, preferences, and motivations. AI-powered tools can sift through resumes, social media profiles, and online engagement patterns, allowing HR professionals to develop a comprehensive profile of their ideal candidate. This data-driven approach enables organizations to segment their target audience effectively, ensuring that messaging is not only relevant but also compelling.

One of the most effective methods for personalizing recruitment campaigns is through the use of targeted content. By utilizing AI algorithms, companies can identify keywords and phrases that resonate with specific demographics or professional backgrounds. For example, a tech company might discover that candidates with a penchant for innovation respond positively to messaging that emphasizes cutting-edge projects and opportunities for professional growth.

By incorporating these insights into job postings and marketing materials, organizations can craft narratives that speak directly to their audience's aspirations and values.

Moreover, AI-driven analytics allows organizations to dynamically adjust their marketing strategies based on real-time feedback. If a particular campaign targeting recent graduates yields lower engagement rates than anticipated, AI tools can quickly analyze the underlying factors—be it the choice of platform, the language used, or even the timing of the outreach. With this data, recruiters can pivot their strategies, experimenting with different messaging or channels to find the most effective combination. This agility is crucial in a job market where candidate preferences can shift rapidly, necessitating a responsive and adaptive recruitment approach.

Another significant advantage of personalized job marketing is the ability to enhance the candidate experience from the first point of contact. AI chatbots, for example, can engage potential applicants on career pages or social media platforms, providing personalized interactions that guide them through the application process. These chatbots can answer common questions, provide insights about company culture, and even suggest roles that align with candidates' skills and interests. This not only streamlines the application process but also makes candidates feel valued and understood, fostering a positive impression of the employer brand.

Social media platforms are also ripe for personalized job marketing campaigns. Advanced AI tools can analyze engagement data to determine which platforms are most frequented by target candidates. For instance, younger candidates may be more active on Instagram and TikTok, while seasoned professionals might frequent LinkedIn. By tailoring content to fit the unique characteristics and preferences of each platform, organizations can ensure their messaging reaches candidates where they are most engaged. Creative formats, such as video job descriptions or employee testimonials, can also be leveraged to create more dynamic content that captures attention and encourages sharing.

Furthermore, leveraging predictive analytics can significantly enhance personalization efforts. By analyzing historical hiring data, AI can predict which candidates are likely to be the best fit for specific roles based on their background, skills, and engagement patterns. This predictive capability enables recruiters to proactively reach out to high-potential candidates with tailored messaging that highlights opportunities relevant to their career paths. For example, if the analysis indicates that candidates from a particular university tend to excel in certain positions, recruiters can design campaigns that specifically target graduates from that institution, emphasizing the unique benefits of joining the organization.

Another innovative approach to personalized job marketing involves the use of immersive technologies such as virtual reality (VR) and augmented reality (AR). These technologies can provide candidates with an interactive experience of the workplace, allowing them to visualize themselves in a potential role and understand company culture in a more engaging way. By integrating these immersive experiences into recruitment campaigns, organizations can create a unique selling proposition that differentiates them from competitors, making the job opportunity more appealing to prospective applicants.

Additionally, AI can support personalized outreach through email marketing campaigns. By segmenting candidates based on their profiles and previous interactions, organizations can send tailored emails that resonate with individual preferences. For instance, a candidate who previously expressed interest in professional development opportunities might receive information about training programs and mentorship initiatives alongside job postings. This level of personalization not only enhances the candidate experience but also reinforces the employer brand as one that genuinely cares about the growth and success of its employees.

Finally, measuring the impact of personalized job marketing campaigns is essential for continuous improvement. AI analytics can provide insights into engagement rates, application conversion rates, and overall effectiveness, allowing organizations to refine their strategies based on what works best.

By tracking key performance indicators (KPIs) such as candidate satisfaction scores, time-to-fill metrics, and quality of hire, recruiters can ensure that their personalized approaches are not just innovative but also effective in achieving hiring goals.

In conclusion, the integration of AI into personalized job marketing campaigns represents a significant advancement in the recruitment landscape. By harnessing the power of data analytics, organizations can craft targeted messages that resonate with potential candidates, enhance their engagement, and ultimately drive higher conversion rates. As the competition for top talent continues to intensify, those organizations that embrace AI-driven personalization will be better positioned to attract and retain the best candidates, fostering a strong employer brand that stands out in the crowded job market.

In the context of AI-driven recruitment strategies, leveraging artificial intelligence to foster diversity and inclusiveness in hiring is not merely a moral imperative; it is a strategic advantage that can enhance an organization's brand and performance. As companies strive to build stronger, more innovative teams, the need for diverse perspectives has become increasingly clear. AI technologies, when applied thoughtfully, can play a pivotal role in creating a more equitable hiring process, helping organizations attract a broader talent pool while mitigating biases that have traditionally plagued recruitment practices.

At the heart of leveraging AI for diverse and inclusive hiring is the ability to analyze vast amounts of data to identify patterns that indicate successful hiring practices. Machine learning algorithms can sift through historical recruitment data to determine which hiring sources and methods yield diverse candidates. By understanding which channels historically attract underrepresented groups, organizations can strategically allocate resources to these avenues. This data-driven approach not only enhances the organization's reach but also ensures that recruitment efforts are targeted and effective.

Furthermore, AI can assist in crafting job descriptions that appeal to a diverse audience. Natural language processing (NLP) tools can analyze the language used in job postings to identify biased or exclusionary terms. For example, certain words may unintentionally signal a preference for a specific demographic or gender. By employing AI tools to optimize language, organizations can create job descriptions that are more inclusive, encouraging a wider range of applicants to apply. This shift in language can significantly impact the diversity of the candidate pool, as it fosters an environment where individuals from various backgrounds feel welcomed and valued.

Once candidates begin to apply, AI can enhance the selection process through unbiased resume screening. Traditional recruitment methods often rely on human judgment, which can be inherently biased. AI algorithms can evaluate resumes based purely on skills and qualifications, effectively minimizing unconscious bias linked to factors such as age, gender, or educational background. By focusing on relevant competencies rather than demographic characteristics, organizations can ensure that candidates are evaluated based on their potential contributions to the company rather than on preconceived notions about their backgrounds.

Moreover, AI-powered assessment tools can be utilized to evaluate candidates' skills and competencies in a standardized manner. These assessments can range from technical skills tests to situational judgment scenarios, allowing candidates from diverse backgrounds to showcase their abilities without the influence of bias. This method not only levels the playing field but also enhances the candidate experience, as individuals can engage with interactive and relevant assessments rather than relying solely on interviews, which can introduce subjective evaluation.

In addition to improving the selection process, AI can play a crucial role in enhancing the overall candidate experience, particularly for underrepresented groups. Chatbots and virtual assistants can provide real-time assistance to candidates, answering questions about the application process, company culture, and diversity initiatives. This interaction not only helps candidates feel more engaged but also demonstrates the organization's commitment to inclusivity. By fostering open lines of communication, organizations can build trust with candidates, making them feel valued and supported throughout the recruitment journey.

However, it is essential to recognize that the implementation of AI in hiring processes is not without its challenges. Organizations must be vigilant in ensuring that the data used to train AI systems is representative of the diverse workforce they aim to cultivate. If historical data reflects biases—such as a lack of diversity within the current workforce—AI algorithms may inadvertently perpetuate these biases. To combat this, organizations should actively seek to diversify their data sources and continuously monitor AI performance to ensure equitable outcomes.

Moreover, transparency is critical in establishing trust with candidates. Organizations should openly communicate how AI systems are utilized in the hiring process, what data is collected, and how decisions are made. This transparency not only empowers candidates but also holds organizations accountable for their hiring practices. By fostering a culture of openness, companies can strengthen their employer brand and enhance their reputation as equitable employers.

In addition, it is imperative for organizations to establish metrics for measuring the effectiveness of their AI-driven recruitment strategies in promoting diversity. By tracking key performance indicators—such as the demographic makeup of candidate pools, the diversity of those hired, and retention rates—companies can assess the impact of their initiatives and make informed adjustments as needed. Regular audits of AI systems can provide insights into potential biases and help organizations refine their strategies to ensure continuous improvement.

As organizations move forward in their journey toward diversity and inclusion, it is crucial to remember that AI is a tool, not a silver bullet. The most effective strategies will integrate AI with human insight and empathy. While AI can streamline processes and offer data-driven insights, it is the human element that ultimately shapes an organization's culture and commitment to diversity. By combining AI capabilities with a genuine commitment to inclusive practices, organizations can foster an environment where diverse talent thrives and contributes to a robust employer brand.

In conclusion, leveraging AI for diverse and inclusive hiring offers a transformative opportunity for organizations to build stronger teams and enhance their employer brand. By utilizing data-driven insights to inform recruitment strategies, crafting inclusive job descriptions, implementing unbiased selection processes, and fostering transparent communication, companies can attract a broader spectrum of talent. Embracing diversity not only enriches the workplace but also drives innovation and enhances overall organizational success. As the landscape of recruitment continues to evolve, organizations that prioritize diversity and inclusion through AI will be well-positioned to thrive in the competitive talent market.

Enhancing Candidate Experience with AI

In today's competitive job market, where candidates are more discerning and have higher expectations than ever, organizations must prioritize the candidate experience as a core component of their employer branding strategy. AI-powered engagement tools have emerged as a transformative force in creating a seamless, interactive, and personalized experience for candidates throughout the recruitment journey. By leveraging these tools, organizations can foster meaningful connections, enhance communication, and ultimately build a stronger employer brand.

One of the most significant advantages of AI in candidate engagement is its ability to facilitate real-time communication. Chatbots, equipped with natural language processing capabilities, have revolutionized the way organizations interact with candidates. These AI-driven tools provide immediate responses to candidate inquiries, whether they are about job descriptions, application statuses, or company culture. By ensuring candidates receive timely information, organizations can significantly reduce anxiety and uncertainty during the application process. This proactive engagement not only reflects positively on the organization but also demonstrates a commitment to transparency and accessibility.

Moreover, chatbots can be programmed to deliver personalized interactions based on candidate profiles. For instance, if a candidate has applied for a specific role, the chatbot can provide tailored insights related to that position, such as information about the team they would be joining or details on the skills and experiences that are particularly valued. This level of personalization not only enhances the candidate experience but also reinforces the employer's brand identity as one that values individual needs and aspirations.

Beyond chatbots, AI-driven engagement tools can also enhance the application process itself. Organizations can utilize AI to streamline application forms by implementing intelligent forms that auto-fill candidate information from LinkedIn or other professional networks. This functionality reduces the time and effort required from candidates, minimizing potential friction points during the application process. When candidates experience a smooth and intuitive application journey, they are more likely to perceive the organization favorably, increasing the likelihood of positive word-of-mouth and enhancing the brand's reputation.

Another critical area where AI engagement tools can make a significant impact is in the realm of feedback and follow-up communication. Traditional recruitment processes often leave candidates in the dark after submitting their applications, leading to frustration and disengagement. AI can change this narrative by automating follow-up communications. For example, once a candidate submits their application, they can receive an automated acknowledgment email, followed by periodic updates on their application status. Such consistent communication not only keeps candidates informed but also reinforces the organization's commitment to a respectful and engaging hiring process.

AI can also assist in gathering feedback from candidates post-interview, a vital step in understanding and improving the candidate experience. By deploying AI-driven surveys that analyze candidate responses, organizations can glean insights into their recruitment process. For instance, they can assess candidates' perceptions of the interview experience, the clarity of communication, and their overall satisfaction. This data can drive continuous improvement efforts, enabling organizations to tailor their recruitment strategies to better meet the expectations and preferences of their candidates.

Furthermore, AI-powered engagement tools can enhance the personalization of content delivered to candidates. Imagine a scenario where candidates receive customized newsletters containing job openings aligned with their skills, interests, and career goals. By utilizing AI algorithms that analyze candidate behavior and preferences, organizations can curate content that resonates with individual candidates. This level of personalization not only keeps candidates engaged but also positions the organization as a thoughtful and innovative employer, further strengthening its employer brand.

The integration of AI in candidate engagement also extends to the use of virtual reality (VR) and augmented reality (AR) technologies, which can create immersive experiences for candidates. For example, organizations can offer virtual office tours or interactive experiences that showcase their company culture and work environment. Candidates can engage with the brand in a dynamic and memorable way, allowing them to envision themselves as part of the organization. Such innovative approaches not only enhance engagement but also differentiate the employer brand in a crowded marketplace.

In addition to enhancing candidate engagement, organizations must also remain vigilant about the ethical implications of AI tools. Ensuring transparency in AI algorithms and maintaining data privacy are paramount in fostering trust with candidates. Organizations should communicate openly about how AI is utilized in the recruitment process and what data is collected. By doing so, they can alleviate concerns candidates may have about surveillance or bias, ultimately reinforcing their reputation as an ethical employer.

As organizations continue to adopt AI-powered engagement tools, measuring the effectiveness of these initiatives becomes essential. Metrics such as candidate satisfaction scores, engagement rates, and application completion rates can provide valuable insights into the impact of AI on the candidate experience. These metrics not only inform recruitment strategies but also serve as benchmarks for continuous improvement in employer branding efforts.

In conclusion, AI-powered engagement tools are redefining the candidate experience, enabling organizations to foster stronger connections, enhance communication, and create a more personalized recruitment journey. By harnessing the capabilities of AI, organizations can not only attract top talent but also position themselves as innovative and thoughtful employers. As the landscape of employer branding continues to evolve, those who prioritize the candidate experience through AI will not only stand out in the marketplace but also cultivate long-term relationships with candidates, ultimately leading to a more robust and authentic employer brand.

In today's competitive job market, candidates expect a seamless and efficient application process that respects their time and effort. Streamlining this process is essential for organizations aiming to enhance candidate experience and secure top talent. Artificial intelligence offers innovative solutions to reduce friction in the application journey, making it not only faster but also more engaging for prospective employees.

At the heart of streamlining the application process is the use of AI-powered chatbots. These virtual assistants can handle routine inquiries about job roles, company culture, and application status 24/7. By integrating chatbots into career pages and application portals, organizations can provide immediate responses to candidates, eliminating the frustration of waiting for human replies. For instance, a candidate may inquire about the specific requirements for a marketing position. The chatbot can promptly provide tailored information, guiding them through the essential criteria and helping them determine if they are a good fit for the role. This immediate feedback not only enhances the candidate experience but also positions the company as responsive and candidate-focused.

Another critical area where AI can streamline the application process is through resume parsing and screening. Traditional methods of reviewing resumes can be labor-intensive and prone to bias, often leading to qualified candidates being overlooked. AI-powered applicant tracking systems (ATS) can automatically parse resumes, extracting key information such as skills, experience, and education. These systems can then rank candidates based on their fit for the job using customized algorithms, allowing recruiters to focus their efforts on the most promising candidates. By minimizing human error and bias in the initial screening phase, organizations can ensure a more equitable hiring process while significantly reducing the time spent on resume reviews.

Moreover, AI algorithms can be designed to learn from previous hiring decisions, continuously improving their ability to identify top talent. By analyzing data from past hires, including performance metrics and retention rates, AI can refine its screening criteria over time. This evolution not only helps in selecting candidates who are more likely to succeed within the organization but also fosters a more data-driven approach to recruitment.

As a result, HR teams can make informed decisions that align with the organization's goals, enhancing the overall quality of hires.

The application process can also benefit from AI-driven personalized experiences. By leveraging data analytics, organizations can deliver tailored application journeys that resonate with individual candidates. For instance, AI can analyze a candidate's profile and past interactions with the organization to suggest specific roles that align with their skills and career aspirations. This level of personalization not only simplifies the application process but also helps candidates feel valued, reinforcing a positive employer brand.

Furthermore, AI can enhance the user interface of application platforms. Intelligent design features, powered by AI, can guide candidates through the application process, offering suggestions and tips at each stage. For example, if a candidate hesitates while filling out a particular section, the AI can provide contextual prompts to clarify requirements. This guidance can significantly reduce candidate drop-off rates, ensuring that more qualified individuals complete their applications.

Another innovative approach to streamlining the application process is through automated video interviews. AI-driven platforms can facilitate initial screening interviews through pre-recorded questions, allowing candidates to respond at their convenience. This flexibility not only accommodates candidates' busy schedules but also allows organizations to assess a larger volume of applicants without overwhelming their HR teams.

AI can analyze these video interviews using natural language processing and facial recognition technology, providing insights into candidates' communication skills and emotional cues. Such tools enable recruiters to identify potential red flags or exceptional candidates early in the process.

While these AI tools significantly enhance the application process, it is essential to maintain a human touch throughout the journey. Candidates still crave connection and rapport, so organizations must strike a balance between automation and personal interaction. After the initial AI-driven interactions, ensuring that a human recruiter follows up with candidates can reinforce a positive experience. This hybrid approach allows candidates to feel supported and understood, further solidifying their interest in the organization.

Additionally, it is crucial to keep candidates informed throughout the application process. AI tools can automate status updates, ensuring that candidates are aware of where they stand in the hiring process without having to reach out for information. Regular communication, whether through automated emails or chatbot interactions, can significantly enhance the candidate experience, reducing anxiety and fostering a sense of transparency.

Feedback loops are another essential component of streamlining the application process. AI tools can gather feedback from candidates post-application, providing valuable insights into their experiences. This data can help organizations identify pain points in their application process, enabling continuous improvement. By acting on candidate feedback, companies can create a more efficient and enjoyable application journey, ultimately attracting and retaining top talent.

As organizations continue to embrace AI in their hiring processes, it is essential to remain vigilant about the ethical implications of these technologies. While AI can mitigate bias in many areas, it is crucial to regularly audit algorithms to ensure they do not inadvertently perpetuate existing inequalities. Organizations must commit to transparency, ensuring that candidates understand how their data is being used and how decisions are made throughout the application process.

Ultimately, streamlining the application process through AI not only enhances the candidate experience but also strengthens employer branding. By creating a more efficient and engaging journey, organizations position themselves as forward-thinking and responsive employers. As candidates increasingly prioritize companies that respect their time and provide seamless interactions, adopting AI-powered solutions becomes imperative for businesses striving to stand out in a crowded talent market. By leveraging the potential of AI, organizations can craft an application experience that is not only efficient but also human-centric, fostering a lasting connection with candidates from the very first interaction.

In the contemporary recruitment landscape, where candidate experience plays an increasingly pivotal role in employer branding, the integration of AI-driven feedback and communication tools has emerged as a game changer. As organizations strive to build authentic connections with potential hires, it is essential to leverage technology to create an engaging and responsive dialogue throughout the recruitment process. AI not only automates but also personalizes interactions, enabling organizations to better understand candidates' needs, preferences, and experiences.

Feedback mechanisms are essential for enhancing candidate experiences. Traditionally, candidates would often submit applications and receive little to no communication about their status, leading to frustration and disengagement. In the AI age, however, recruiters can employ chatbots and automated messaging systems to offer real-time updates, ensuring candidates feel acknowledged and valued. These AI-powered tools can provide information on the next steps in the hiring process, answer frequently asked questions, and even offer insights into the company culture, all of which contribute to a more transparent and engaging experience.

Moreover, AI can facilitate a two-way communication channel. By enabling candidates to provide feedback on their experience, organizations can gain valuable insights into their recruitment processes. For instance, after an interview, an AI system could send a brief survey to candidates, asking them about their perceptions of the interview, the clarity of communication, and any areas for improvement. This feedback loop not only demonstrates to candidates that their opinions are valued but also allows organizations to refine their processes continually. By analyzing the aggregated responses, companies can identify trends and areas needing attention, which ultimately leads to a more positive candidate experience.

The use of natural language processing (NLP) further enhances communication efforts. NLP algorithms can analyze candidates' written responses in surveys or feedback forms, extracting sentiment and emotional tone. This analysis enables recruiters to gauge candidates' satisfaction levels, pinpointing any potential issues that may arise during the process. For instance, if a significant number of candidates express confusion regarding the interview scheduling process, organizations can address this gap, ensuring future candidates are better informed. This proactive approach not only reduces candidate drop-off rates but also bolsters the employer brand by showcasing a commitment to continuous improvement.

Furthermore, personalized communication fueled by AI can significantly enhance the candidate experience. By utilizing data from candidates' profiles, AI systems can tailor messages to resonate more deeply with individual candidates. For instance, if a candidate has expressed a particular interest in professional development opportunities, automated communication can highlight relevant training programs and career progression paths within the organization. This level of personalization not only reflects a candidate's value to the organization but also fosters a sense of belonging and alignment with the company's mission.

AI also enables organizations to segment candidates based on their interactions and feedback. By categorizing candidates according to their stage in the recruitment process, the organization can tailor its communication strategies to each group. For example, candidates who have recently interviewed may receive follow-up messages within a specific timeframe, while those who have been rejected can receive constructive feedback that can aid their future applications. By demonstrating a thoughtful and tailored approach, organizations can maintain positive relationships with candidates, even those who were not ultimately selected.

In addition to improving feedback and communication, AI can streamline the entire recruitment process, enhancing the candidate experience. For instance, AI-driven platforms can analyze candidate profiles and match them with job openings based on skills, experience, and preferences. This matching process not only speeds up the recruitment cycle but also ensures that candidates are directed towards roles that align with their career aspirations. This targeted approach minimizes the chances of candidates applying for positions that do not suit their skills or ambitions, ultimately leading to higher satisfaction rates.

Moreover, the integration of AI into communication strategies can impart a sense of urgency and responsiveness that candidates appreciate. Automated systems can ensure that candidates receive timely notifications about their application status, interview schedules, or any required follow-up actions. The efficiency of AI allows organizations to maintain a high level of engagement without overwhelming their HR teams. This balance of automation and human touch is crucial, as candidates still value personal interactions and empathy throughout the journey.

Considering the ongoing evolution of technology, organizations must remain vigilant about the ethical implications of AI in recruitment communication. While AI can enhance feedback mechanisms and streamline processes, the application of these tools should prioritize data privacy and the protection of candidates' information. Organizations must be transparent about how data is collected, used, and stored, and they must ensure that candidates consent to this process. Additionally, addressing biases embedded within AI algorithms is critical. Organizations should actively monitor AI systems to prevent perpetuating existing biases, ensuring that all candidates are treated fairly and equitably.

As organizations embrace AI to enhance candidate experience, they must also be prepared for the continuous evolution of these technologies. Regularly assessing the performance of AI-driven communication tools is essential to ensure they meet the changing needs of candidates.

As the workforce evolves, so too should the strategies employed by organizations to engage and communicate with potential hires.

In conclusion, AI-driven feedback and communication mechanisms are pivotal in enhancing candidate experiences in the recruitment process. By creating a responsive, personalized, and transparent dialogue, organizations can foster a sense of connection and engagement with candidates. This not only improves the overall candidate experience but also strengthens the employer brand, positioning organizations as forward-thinking, empathetic, and committed to attracting top talent. As the recruitment landscape continues to evolve, those who prioritize candidate experience through innovative AI solutions will undoubtedly stand out in the competitive talent marketplace.

Building Authentic Employer Brands with AI Insights

In an era where authenticity and transparency are paramount, organizations must embrace data-driven storytelling as a crucial component of their employer branding strategy. Brand storytelling is the art of weaving narratives that resonate with target audiences, and when infused with data, it transforms into a powerful tool for conveying a company's ethos, culture, and values. Leveraging AI and analytics in this process allows organizations to craft narratives that are not only compelling but also backed by insights that reflect the true employee experience.

The journey begins with a comprehensive understanding of the workforce's perceptions and sentiments. AI-powered analytics tools can sift through vast amounts of data gathered from various sources, including employee feedback, social media interactions, and online reviews. By employing natural language processing (NLP), organizations can analyze text data to identify common themes in employee experiences, values, and expectations. This analysis provides a wealth of information that can inform brand narratives and ensure they align with the authentic employee journey.

For instance, if data reveals that employees value collaboration and innovation, these themes can be woven into the brand narrative. A company might highlight their open-office layout, cross-departmental projects, or innovation labs as part of their storytelling. Instead of merely stating that the organization values teamwork, the narrative can include specific examples and testimonials from employees who have thrived in collaborative environments. This not only enhances authenticity but also provides potential candidates with relatable insights into the company culture.

Another critical aspect of data-driven storytelling is the personalization of narratives. AI enables organizations to segment audiences based on various factors such as demographics, career stages, and professional interests. By understanding the unique preferences and motivations of different segments, companies can tailor their stories to resonate more effectively. For example, a company targeting recent graduates may emphasize mentorship programs and career development opportunities, while a narrative aimed at seasoned professionals might spotlight leadership roles and strategic challenges.

Moreover, platforms powered by AI can facilitate this personalized storytelling through dynamic content delivery. For instance, a company's career page could adapt its messaging based on the visitor's profile, showcasing specific employee testimonials, success stories, and relevant content that speaks directly to the visitor's interests. This level of personalization not only captures attention but also fosters a deeper connection between the potential candidate and the employer brand.

Visual storytelling is another avenue where data-driven insights can play a pivotal role. Visual content, such as videos, infographics, and images, can be crafted using insights derived from employee stories and experiences. For instance, organizations can create video testimonials where employees share their journeys and experiences within the company. AI can help identify impactful quotes and moments from these stories, ensuring the final product resonates with viewers.

Additionally, by analyzing engagement metrics of previous visual content, organizations can refine their storytelling approach. If a particular type of video content garners higher engagement on social media, it may indicate the themes or formats that resonate most with the audience. For example, if behind-the-scenes glimpses into day-to-day operations receive more views, companies could consider producing a series of such videos to build a more authentic image.

Furthermore, using AI to monitor and analyze competitors' employer branding strategies can provide valuable insights. By tapping into available data on competitor brands, organizations can identify gaps in their storytelling and capitalize on unique differentiators. If a competitor is emphasizing flexibility and remote work options, a company can craft narratives that highlight their own innovative work arrangements and employee-centric policies, thus positioning themselves as a more attractive option in the talent marketplace.

The effectiveness of data-driven storytelling can also be evaluated through continuous feedback mechanisms. AI tools can enable organizations to gather real-time feedback on their employer branding initiatives, allowing for quick adjustments based on audience reactions. Surveys, polls, and sentiment analysis can gauge how current and potential employees perceive the brand's narrative. This iterative process ensures that storytelling remains relevant and reflective of the evolving employee experience.

To illustrate the impact of data-driven brand storytelling, consider the case of a technology firm that successfully transformed its employer brand through analytics. Initially struggling with a perception of being overly corporate and rigid, the company utilized AI-powered sentiment analysis to understand employee sentiments and values. They discovered that employees valued creativity and a dynamic work environment. Using these insights, the firm pivoted its storytelling to highlight projects that showcased innovation and employee creativity, along with testimonials from team members who thrived in this environment.

The results were profound: the company not only attracted a more diverse pool of applicants but also saw improved employee engagement and retention rates. Employees felt a deeper connection to the brand, as they saw their values reflected in the stories being told. This case exemplifies how data-driven brand storytelling can lead to transformative results when aligned with organizational values and employee experiences.

In conclusion, data-driven brand storytelling is an essential strategy for organizations looking to build an authentic employer brand that resonates with prospective and existing employees alike. By harnessing the power of AI and analytics, businesses can craft narratives that are not only compelling but also reflective of the genuine employee experience. Personalization, visual storytelling, competitive analysis, and continuous feedback are integral components of this approach, ensuring that the employer brand remains vibrant, relevant, and aligned with the aspirations of the workforce. In the quest for top talent, it is the organizations that tell the most authentic and relatable stories that will stand out in an increasingly competitive landscape.

In the quest to craft an authentic employer brand, understanding brand perception is paramount. This understanding is further augmented by the capabilities of artificial intelligence (AI), which provides a nuanced lens through which organizations can gauge how they are viewed by both current and potential employees. By employing AI-driven tools and methodologies, HR professionals and organizational leaders can harness vast amounts of data to derive actionable insights, ultimately enhancing their employer branding strategies.

The first step in measuring brand perception through AI is to leverage sentiment analysis. This technique utilizes natural language processing (NLP) algorithms to analyze text data from various sources such as social media, employee reviews on platforms like Glassdoor, and even internal feedback mechanisms. By assessing the sentiment expressed in these texts, organizations can identify prevailing attitudes towards their brand. For instance, if a significant number of employee reviews highlight a positive work culture but express frustration about career advancement opportunities, this insight can inform targeted branding initiatives that address these gaps. AI tools can not only quantify these sentiments but also categorize them, allowing HR teams to pinpoint specific areas of strength and weakness in their employer branding.

Additionally, AI can enhance traditional survey methodologies, transforming how organizations collect and analyze feedback. Rather than relying solely on annual employee engagement surveys, organizations can implement AI-driven pulse surveys that are deployed more frequently, capturing real-time data on employee sentiment. These surveys can employ algorithms that analyze responses for trends and anomalies, providing immediate insights into how employees perceive various aspects of the organizational culture. By continuously monitoring these perceptions, businesses can react swiftly to any shifts, ensuring that their employer brand remains aligned with employee expectations and industry standards.

Another vital dimension of measuring brand perception involves understanding the candidate experience during the recruitment process. AI can analyze candidate interactions across various touchpoints—job postings, application processes, interviews, and onboarding—to gauge their perceptions and feelings about the brand. For instance, chatbots powered by AI can conduct post-interview surveys, collecting feedback on the candidates' experiences. By processing this data, organizations can identify pain points in their recruitment process, such as lengthy application forms or a lack of communication, and make the necessary adjustments to enhance the overall candidate experience. In this way, AI not only measures perceptions but actively contributes to the evolution of the employer brand.

Moreover, social listening tools powered by AI can provide insights into how a brand is perceived externally. By monitoring conversations on social media platforms, forums, and review sites, organizations can gauge public sentiment about their brand in real-time. AI algorithms can detect shifts in perception, allowing businesses to respond proactively to negative comments or misinformation. For example, if a particular campaign draws criticism or if employees express dissatisfaction publicly, organizations can address these issues promptly, demonstrating a commitment to transparency and improvement. This responsiveness not only protects the brand but can also enhance its authenticity in the eyes of current and prospective employees.

The integration of AI also enables organizations to benchmark their employer brand against competitors. AI tools can aggregate data from various sources, allowing HR professionals to analyze how their brand perception stacks up against industry peers. This competitive analysis can reveal critical insights into what attracts talent in the industry and how organizations can differentiate themselves. For instance, if a competitor is gaining traction among job seekers due to a robust diversity and inclusion strategy, this insight can prompt similar initiatives within the organization, thereby enhancing its employer brand and ensuring its relevance in the talent market.

Furthermore, AI analytics can aid in the visualization of brand perception data, transforming complex datasets into intuitive dashboards that provide a clear overview of key metrics. These visualizations can highlight trends over time, such as shifts in employee or candidate sentiment, enabling stakeholders to make data-driven decisions about their employer branding strategies. By presenting this information in an accessible format, organizations can engage leaders from various departments, fostering a culture of collaboration and shared accountability in enhancing the employer brand.

Another innovative approach to measuring brand perception involves the use of machine learning algorithms to segment employee and candidate data. By identifying distinct personas—such as high performers, new hires, or long-tenured employees—organizations can tailor their branding initiatives to resonate with each group. For example, insights gained from analyzing the experiences of new hires can inform onboarding processes, while feedback from seasoned employees can guide leadership development programs. This targeted approach ensures that the employer brand speaks authentically to diverse employee experiences, reinforcing its overall credibility.

However, it is essential to recognize the ethical implications of employing AI in measuring brand perception. As organizations tap into vast datasets, they must navigate concerns related to data privacy and consent. Transparency in how data is collected and analyzed is crucial for building trust among employees and candidates. Organizations should ensure that AI tools are used responsibly, with safeguards in place to protect individual privacy. By prioritizing ethical considerations, businesses can enhance their employer brand, fostering a culture of trust and integrity.

In conclusion, measuring brand perception through AI offers organizations a comprehensive framework for understanding how they are viewed by current and potential employees. By leveraging sentiment analysis, real-time feedback mechanisms, social listening tools, and competitive benchmarking, businesses can gain valuable insights that inform their employer branding strategies. The integration of AI not only enhances the precision of these measurements but also fosters a proactive approach to managing brand perception. As organizations navigate the complexities of the talent landscape, those that harness the power of AI to understand and enhance their employer brand will be better positioned to attract, engage, and retain top talent in an increasingly competitive market. Through the thoughtful application of AI, businesses can create an authentic employer brand that resonates with employees, ultimately driving organizational success.

In the realm of employer branding, artificial intelligence (AI) has emerged as a transformative force, enabling organizations to create more authentic and resonant brand identities. This section delves into compelling case studies that exemplify the effective use of AI in building authentic employer brands. These examples not only showcase the successful implementation of AI-powered strategies but also provide valuable insights into the process of aligning technology with human-centric principles.

One notable case is that of Unilever, the multinational consumer goods company, which has leveraged AI to reshape its recruitment process. Facing challenges in attracting diverse talent and optimizing its hiring efficiency, Unilever turned to a combination of AI-driven assessments and data analytics. The company implemented an AI-powered recruitment platform that utilized gamified assessments to evaluate candidates' skills and cultural fit. This platform not only streamlined the application process but also helped eliminate bias by focusing on candidates' abilities rather than their resumes.

The results were impressive. Unilever reported a significant increase in the diversity of its candidate pool, with the gamified assessments attracting candidates from various backgrounds. The company also noted a reduction in hiring time and improved candidate experience, as applicants appreciated the interactive format of the assessments. By employing AI thoughtfully, Unilever not only attracted top talent but also reinforced its commitment to diversity and inclusion, ultimately solidifying its employer brand as an innovative and forward-thinking organization.

Another striking example comes from Hilton Worldwide, which utilized AI to enhance its employer branding through personalized career experiences. Recognizing that job seekers are increasingly looking for tailored engagement, Hilton introduced an AI chatbot named "Connie." This smart assistant was designed to interact with potential candidates on the company's career site, providing real-time responses to inquiries about job roles, company culture, and application processes. Connie was trained on a wealth of information about Hilton's values, benefits, and career paths, enabling her to deliver personalized insights based on individual user profiles.

The impact of Connie was profound. Hilton witnessed a notable increase in candidate engagement rates, with users spending significantly more time on the career site and showing a higher interest in available positions. By integrating AI into the candidate experience, Hilton not only improved its recruitment metrics but also enhanced its employer brand perception as a company that values innovation and candidate-centric approaches.

In the technology sector, IBM stands out with its AI-driven employee feedback and engagement platform, Watson Talent. The platform leverages natural language processing and machine learning to analyze employee sentiment and engagement levels in real time. By collecting data from various employee interactions—such as surveys, emails, and performance reviews—IBM can gain insights into employee experiences, identify areas for improvement, and tailor its employer branding strategies accordingly.

This commitment to understanding and responding to employee feedback has resulted in a more authentic employer brand for IBM. Employees feel heard and valued, which not only boosts morale but also enhances the company's reputation as a desirable workplace. By utilizing AI to create a feedback loop that informs their branding efforts, IBM has successfully established itself as a leader in fostering a culture of transparency and inclusivity.

A more recent example involves the financial services firm, American Express. In its quest to attract younger talent, American Express implemented an AI-powered social media strategy that analyzed trends and preferences among Generation Z. By utilizing predictive analytics, the company was able to create targeted content that resonated with this demographic. The AI system identified the types of messages, visuals, and themes that engaged potential candidates, enabling American Express to craft a compelling narrative around its employer brand.

The outcome was a significant uptick in engagement rates on social media platforms, particularly among younger users. The strategic use of AI allowed American Express to position itself as a modern, inclusive, and innovative employer, effectively bridging the gap between traditional financial services and the expectations of a new generation of talent.

Moreover, the global technology company Siemens has made remarkable strides in utilizing AI for employer branding. Siemens deployed AI-driven analytics to assess its employer brand perception across various regions and demographics. By analyzing social media sentiment, employee reviews, and other data points, Siemens was able to pinpoint specific areas where its branding efforts could be enhanced.

One particularly successful initiative was Siemens' "Make Your Mark" campaign, which leveraged AI to identify key themes that resonated with potential candidates. The campaign not only highlighted the company's commitment to innovation and sustainability but also showcased employee stories that reflected diverse experiences and backgrounds. By creating a campaign rooted in real employee narratives, Siemens effectively humanized its brand, making it more relatable and appealing to prospective talent.

These case studies collectively illustrate the myriad ways in which AI can be harnessed to build authentic employer brands. Each organization, through its unique challenges and strategies, has demonstrated that AI is not merely a tool for efficiency; it is a powerful ally in cultivating brand authenticity and resonance.

As evidenced by Unilever, Hilton, IBM, American Express, and Siemens, the key to leveraging AI for employer branding lies in a deep understanding of both the technology and the human elements of branding. By integrating AI insights with genuine employee experiences and values, organizations can create compelling narratives that resonate with candidates and employees alike.

The journey towards building an authentic employer brand is ongoing, and as AI continues to evolve, so too will the opportunities for organizations to refine their branding strategies. In this rapidly changing landscape, the successful integration of AI into employer branding efforts is not just a matter of staying competitive; it is an essential step towards creating workplaces that are vibrant, inclusive, and aligned with the aspirations of a diverse workforce.

Engaging and Retaining Talent Using AI

In the contemporary workplace, the onboarding and development of employees have taken on a new significance, particularly in the context of an increasingly competitive talent landscape. As organizations strive to engage and retain top talent, the integration of artificial intelligence (AI) into these processes offers a transformative approach that not only enhances efficiency but also enriches the employee experience. By harnessing AI, organizations can create personalized onboarding journeys and foster continuous development, driving both employee satisfaction and long-term loyalty.

The onboarding process is critical in setting the tone for a new hire's experience within an organization. Historically, onboarding has often been a cumbersome and disjointed affair, characterized by overwhelming paperwork, inconsistent training, and a lack of personalized engagement. However, AI is revolutionizing this process, enabling organizations to create tailored onboarding programs that resonate deeply with new employees. Through the analysis of data from past onboarding experiences, AI can identify best practices and optimize the onboarding journey based on individual employee profiles.

AI can facilitate an engaging onboarding experience through chatbots and virtual assistants that guide new hires through the necessary steps. These intelligent tools can provide real-time answers to common questions, assist with paperwork, and offer insights into company culture. By utilizing natural language processing, these AI-driven solutions can engage employees in conversational interactions, making them feel supported and valued from day one. This personalized approach significantly reduces the time spent on administrative tasks, allowing HR professionals to focus on strategic initiatives that enhance the overall employee experience.

Moreover, AI can analyze the effectiveness of various onboarding strategies by collecting feedback in real time. Machine learning algorithms can process this feedback to identify patterns and areas for improvement. For instance, if a significant number of new hires report confusion about specific company policies, AI can highlight these areas for HR to refine and clarify, thereby continuously improving the onboarding process for future employees. This iterative feedback loop not only enhances the onboarding experience but also demonstrates to new hires that the organization is committed to their integration and success.

As new employees settle into their roles, ongoing development becomes paramount. AI-powered learning management systems (LMS) can facilitate continuous professional growth tailored to each employee's unique needs and career aspirations. By leveraging data analytics, these systems can assess an employee's skills, preferences, and performance metrics to curate personalized training programs. This approach ensures that employees are not subjected to a one-size-fits-all training regimen but instead receive targeted content that aligns with their career goals and the organization's objectives.

Furthermore, AI can enhance the development process by providing predictive insights into employee performance and potential career trajectories. By analyzing historical data, AI can identify high-potential employees and suggest pathways for advancement. Organizations can create tailored development plans that include mentorship opportunities, skill-building workshops, and cross-functional projects, all guided by the insights generated through AI. This proactive approach not only fosters employee engagement but also cultivates a culture of growth and innovation within the organization.

Another significant advantage of integrating AI into employee development is the ability to monitor progress and provide real-time feedback. Traditional performance review processes often rely on annual or biannual evaluations, which may not accurately reflect an employee's ongoing contributions and growth. AI-driven platforms can offer continuous performance tracking, allowing managers to provide timely feedback and recognize achievements as they occur. This approach empowers employees to take ownership of their development journey, fostering a sense of accountability and motivation.

Moreover, AI can facilitate peer learning and collaboration among employees, creating a more interconnected workplace. By analyzing employee interactions and performance metrics, AI can identify opportunities for collaboration and suggest team formations based on complementary skills. For example, an AI system might recommend pairing a seasoned developer with a new recruit who is eager to learn, resulting in a mutually beneficial relationship that enhances both parties' skill sets. This collaborative environment not only bolsters employee engagement but also drives innovation as diverse perspectives come together to solve complex challenges.

As organizations increasingly embrace remote and hybrid work models, the role of AI in employee onboarding and development becomes even more critical. Virtual onboarding programs powered by AI can bridge the gap between in-person and remote experiences, ensuring that new hires feel connected and engaged regardless of their physical location. Through virtual reality (VR) and augmented reality (AR) technologies, organizations can create immersive training experiences that simulate real-world scenarios, enabling employees to practice skills in a safe environment before applying them in their roles.

Additionally, AI can assist in creating a sense of community among remote employees. Social collaboration tools driven by AI can recommend networking opportunities, interest-based groups, and professional development events, fostering connections that may otherwise be difficult to establish in a remote setting. By facilitating these interactions, organizations can cultivate a strong organizational culture that supports employee engagement and retention, even in a dispersed workforce.

In conclusion, the integration of AI in employee onboarding and development represents a significant shift in how organizations approach talent management. By leveraging AI-driven insights, organizations can create personalized onboarding experiences that resonate with new hires, fostering a sense of belonging and commitment from the outset. Coupled with ongoing development opportunities tailored to individual needs and performance, AI empowers organizations to cultivate a workforce that is not only engaged but also equipped to thrive in an ever-evolving business landscape. As companies continue to navigate the complexities of talent management, embracing AI as a core component of their onboarding and development strategies will prove essential in attracting, engaging, and retaining top talent.

In today's dynamic work environment, engaging and retaining top talent is crucial for organizational success. With the advent of artificial intelligence, HR professionals have new opportunities to proactively address employee retention through predictive strategies that leverage data-driven insights. By harnessing the power of AI, organizations can not only anticipate potential turnover but also develop tailored interventions that enhance employee satisfaction and loyalty.

Predictive retention strategies employ advanced algorithms and machine learning models to analyze a wide array of data points related to employee behavior and engagement. This data can include everything from performance metrics and employee feedback to external market trends. By analyzing this information, organizations can identify warning signs that may indicate an employee is at risk of leaving, allowing them to take timely and decisive action.

One of the key components of predictive retention strategies is the use of employee engagement surveys. Traditionally, these surveys have been conducted annually, often resulting in outdated data that fails to reflect the current mood of the workforce. However, with AI-driven tools, organizations can conduct real-time sentiment analysis to gauge employee feelings more accurately and frequently. Natural language processing (NLP) techniques can analyze open-ended responses, providing deeper insights into the specific factors that contribute to employee satisfaction or dissatisfaction. This continuous feedback loop allows HR teams to address issues proactively, fostering a more engaged workforce.

Another vital aspect of predictive retention involves the combination of demographic data with performance metrics. AI tools can uncover patterns that might not be immediately obvious, such as correlations between specific demographics and turnover rates. For instance, organizations might discover that employees in particular age groups or with specific skill sets are more likely to leave within a certain timeframe. By understanding these patterns, HR professionals can develop targeted retention strategies, such as mentorship programs for younger employees or career development initiatives for those whose skills are in demand.

Furthermore, predictive analytics can enhance the onboarding process, which is often a critical period for new hires. Research consistently shows that employees who have a positive onboarding experience are more likely to remain with an organization long-term. AI can facilitate personalized onboarding experiences by analyzing the unique needs and preferences of each new employee. For example, AI-powered platforms can recommend tailored training modules based on an employee's prior experience, learning style, and career aspirations. By investing in a customized onboarding process, organizations can cultivate a sense of belonging and alignment with their employer brand from the very start.

Retention strategies can also benefit from the integration of AI-powered chatbots. These digital assistants can provide real-time support and information to employees, answering questions about benefits, career progression, and company policies. By offering immediate assistance, chatbots enhance employee experiences and foster a culture of open communication. Additionally, they can collect valuable feedback on employee concerns and suggestions, feeding this data back into the predictive analytics engine. This creates a virtuous cycle where employee insights inform retention strategies, and those strategies, in turn, improve employee satisfaction.

Moreover, AI can play a pivotal role in identifying and nurturing high-potential employees. Through performance evaluations and skill assessments, AI systems can flag individuals who demonstrate leadership potential or possess critical skills that align with future organizational needs. By recognizing these employees early on, organizations can implement tailored development programs, such as leadership training, mentorship opportunities, or cross-departmental projects. This not only helps retain top talent but also prepares the workforce for future challenges and opportunities.

However, while predictive retention strategies present numerous advantages, they also raise ethical considerations that organizations must navigate carefully. The reliance on data can inadvertently lead to biases, particularly if the underlying data is not diverse or representative. To mitigate this risk, organizations should ensure that their data sources are inclusive and that their AI models are regularly audited for fairness. Additionally, transparency with employees regarding how their data is used can build trust and foster a culture of collaboration.

As organizations implement predictive retention strategies, it is vital to maintain a human-centric approach. While AI can provide invaluable insights, it is ultimately the human element—empathy, understanding, and connection—that drives employee engagement and satisfaction. HR professionals should view AI as a tool that augments their capabilities rather than replaces them. By combining data-driven insights with personal interactions, organizations can create a supportive environment that encourages employees to thrive.

The effectiveness of predictive retention strategies can be

further enhanced by integrating them with broader employee engagement initiatives. For instance, organizations can use insights gained from predictive analytics to inform their employee development programs, workplace wellness initiatives, and recognition efforts. By creating a holistic approach to employee engagement that incorporates predictive strategies, organizations can foster a culture of continuous improvement and adaptability.

In summary, the application of predictive retention strategies through AI is a game-changer for organizations seeking to engage and retain their top talent. By leveraging data-driven insights, HR professionals can proactively identify at-risk employees, personalize onboarding experiences, and nurture high-potential individuals. However, it is essential to balance these strategies with ethical considerations and a human-centric approach. By doing so, organizations can cultivate an environment where employees feel valued, supported, and motivated to contribute to their employer's success, ultimately leading to a stronger, more resilient brand.

In the rapidly evolving landscape of employer branding, the integration of artificial intelligence presents unique opportunities to create a human-centric workplace that prioritizes employee engagement and retention. While AI technologies are often perceived as cold or impersonal, they can be harnessed to foster a more inclusive, supportive, and empathetic work environment.

By strategically implementing AI tools, organizations can enhance the employee experience, ensuring that employees feel valued and connected to the company's mission and values.

One of the primary ways AI can contribute to a human-centric workplace is through personalized employee journeys. Traditional HR processes often follow a one-size-fits-all approach, which can lead to disengagement among employees who feel their unique needs are not being met. AI-powered tools can assess individual employee preferences, strengths, and aspirations, enabling HR professionals to tailor development paths and career opportunities accordingly. For instance, machine learning algorithms can analyze employee data to identify patterns and recommend personalized learning and development programs that align with each employee's career goals. This targeted approach not only enhances skill acquisition but also demonstrates a commitment to employee growth, fostering loyalty and retention.

Moreover, AI-driven sentiment analysis tools can provide valuable insights into employee morale and engagement levels. By analyzing feedback from surveys, performance reviews, and even informal communication channels, AI can help organizations identify areas where employees may feel undervalued or disengaged. For example, if sentiment analysis reveals that remote employees are feeling isolated, organizations can take proactive measures to enhance virtual team-building activities or improve communication tools.

By addressing employee concerns in real time, organizations can cultivate a more engaged workforce that feels heard and appreciated.

AI also plays a crucial role in facilitating ongoing feedback and performance management. Traditional performance reviews, often conducted annually, can feel disconnected from employees' day-to-day experiences. By leveraging AI tools that enable continuous feedback and real-time performance tracking, organizations can create a culture of open communication and ongoing development. Performance management platforms equipped with AI can prompt managers to provide immediate feedback on projects, fostering a more dynamic and responsive environment. This continuous dialogue not only helps employees understand their contributions in real time but also reinforces a culture of recognition and appreciation, leading to higher job satisfaction.

In addition to enhancing individual employee experiences, AI can also facilitate team dynamics and collaboration. AI-driven collaboration tools can analyze team interactions, identifying patterns that either promote or hinder effective teamwork. For instance, these tools can suggest optimal team compositions based on complementary skills, past performance data, and project requirements. By creating balanced, diverse teams, organizations can harness the strengths of their employees, leading to more innovative solutions and greater job satisfaction.

Furthermore, AI can help manage workflows and communication, ensuring that team members are aligned and informed, which is essential for maintaining a sense of connection in a hybrid work environment.

Moreover, the integration of AI in employee engagement initiatives can help organizations foster a sense of purpose and belonging among their workforce. AI can analyze employee interests and values, aligning them with organizational goals and missions. For example, AI algorithms can identify employees who are passionate about sustainability and connect them with projects or initiatives that focus on environmental responsibility. By aligning individual passions with organizational objectives, companies not only enhance employee engagement but also cultivate a deeper connection to the brand, reinforcing the idea that employees are integral to the organization's mission.

However, to truly create a human-centric AI workplace, organizations must prioritize ethical considerations in their use of AI technologies. Transparency in how AI systems operate and the data they collect is critical to building trust among employees. Organizations should communicate clearly about the purpose of AI tools, how employee data will be used, and the measures in place to protect privacy. Establishing an ethical framework for AI usage can prevent potential backlash and ensure that employees view these technologies as supportive rather than intrusive.

Furthermore, organizations must remain vigilant about the potential for bias in AI algorithms. AI systems are only as good as the data they are trained on, and if that data reflects existing biases, the outcomes can perpetuate inequalities within the workplace. To mitigate this risk, organizations need to continuously monitor AI tools for fairness and inclusivity, ensuring that they promote equity in opportunities and experiences. In doing so, organizations can foster a workplace culture that values diversity and inclusion, essential components of a human-centric environment.

Finally, creating a human-centric AI workplace requires ongoing commitment and adaptability. As technology evolves, so too should the strategies organizations employ to engage and retain their talent. Regularly soliciting employee feedback on AI tools and initiatives allows organizations to refine their approaches and ensure they remain aligned with employee needs. By fostering a culture of agility and responsiveness, organizations can cultivate a workplace environment that is not only technologically advanced but also deeply human-centered.

In conclusion, the integration of AI into the workplace offers a transformative opportunity for organizations to enhance employee engagement and retention. By leveraging AI tools to personalize employee experiences, facilitate open communication, and align individual goals with organizational objectives, companies can create a human-centric environment that fosters loyalty and satisfaction. With a commitment to ethical practices and a focus on inclusivity, organizations can navigate the complexities of a rapidly changing workforce landscape, ultimately building a stronger, more resilient employer brand. This human-centric approach not only positions organizations as attractive employers but also cultivates a thriving workplace culture that empowers employees to flourish.

Navigating Ethical Considerations in AI Employer Branding

As organizations increasingly rely on artificial intelligence to enhance their employer branding strategies, the ethical implications surrounding data privacy and security become paramount. The integration of AI into recruitment and employee engagement processes often involves the collection, analysis, and storage of vast amounts of data—much of which is personal and sensitive. This necessitates a thorough understanding of the legal, ethical, and practical dimensions of data privacy to safeguard both candidates and employees while ensuring compliance with relevant regulations.

The legal landscape regarding data privacy has evolved significantly in recent years, influenced by heightened public awareness and regulatory scrutiny. Frameworks such as the General Data Protection Regulation (GDPR) in Europe and the California Consumer Privacy Act (CCPA) in the United States have set stringent guidelines on how organizations can collect and process personal data. These regulations emphasize the necessity for transparency, consent, and the right to access information. As HR professionals and organizational leaders harness AI tools for employer branding, they must ensure that their practices align with these legal requirements.

At the core of ethical data handling lies the principle of informed consent. Candidates and employees must be made aware of how their data will be used, who will have access to it, and the measures in place to protect it. Organizations should prioritize clear communication regarding data collection practices, explaining how AI technologies analyze data to enhance recruitment processes or improve employee experiences. For instance, when utilizing AI-driven chatbots for candidate interactions, companies should disclose that data from these conversations may be used to improve the chatbot's performance or enhance the recruitment process. This transparency not only fosters trust but also empowers individuals to make informed decisions about their data.

In addition to informed consent, organizations must implement robust data security measures to protect sensitive information from unauthorized access or breaches. The increased reliance on AI systems can introduce vulnerabilities, as these systems may be targeted by cybercriminals seeking to exploit personal data. Therefore, HR professionals must collaborate with IT and cybersecurity teams to establish comprehensive data protection protocols. This includes employing encryption technologies, conducting regular security audits, and ensuring that all employees involved in data handling are trained in best practices for data security.

Furthermore, organizations should adopt a data minimization principle, collecting only the information necessary for employer branding efforts. By limiting the data collected to what is essential, companies reduce the risk of exposure in the event of a data breach and enhance their reputation as responsible data stewards. For instance, if an AI recruitment tool requires demographic information for diversity metrics, organizations should evaluate whether such data is critical for their branding goals and whether it can be anonymized to protect individual identities.

The ethical use of AI extends beyond compliance with legal requirements; it also encompasses the need to mitigate bias and ensure fairness in AI algorithms. As AI systems learn from historical data, there is a risk that they may inadvertently perpetuate existing biases present in that data. This can lead to discrimination in recruitment processes, undermining the very goals of diversity and inclusion that many organizations strive to achieve. Therefore, it is essential for HR leaders to regularly audit AI algorithms to identify and address potential biases. Implementing fairness assessments and utilizing diverse training datasets can help organizations create more equitable AI systems that reflect a commitment to ethical employer branding.

Moreover, organizations should establish clear policies regarding data retention and deletion. While AI systems may require historical data for analysis and predictive modeling, it is crucial to define how long personal data will be stored and when it will be deleted. Adopting a transparent data retention policy not only ensures compliance with legal frameworks but also reinforces a culture of respect for individual privacy. Employees and candidates are more likely to engage with organizations that demonstrate a commitment to responsible data management, further strengthening the employer brand.

In addition to these operational considerations, organizations should actively engage with their employees and candidates about data privacy practices. Soliciting feedback on data handling practices can foster a sense of collaboration and trust. Furthermore, organizations can establish advisory boards or focus groups to discuss data privacy concerns and trends in AI. By involving diverse perspectives in the dialogue around data privacy, companies can better align their employer branding strategies with the expectations and values of their workforce.

As the landscape of employer branding continues to evolve with AI, organizations must remain vigilant in addressing the ethical considerations surrounding data privacy and security. The implementation of ethical data practices not only protects individuals but also enhances the organization's reputation, positioning it as a leader in responsible employer branding. By prioritizing transparency, security, fairness, and employee engagement, businesses can leverage AI to create a strong, authentic employer brand that resonates with both potential and existing employees.

In conclusion, navigating the complexities of data privacy and security in the context of AI employer branding requires a multifaceted approach. By embracing legal compliance, fostering transparency, implementing robust security measures, addressing bias, and engaging with stakeholders, organizations can harness the power of AI while upholding the ethical standards that are increasingly demanded by today's workforce. As businesses strive to attract and retain top talent, prioritizing ethical data practices will not only safeguard their reputation but also create a more inclusive and trustworthy employer brand.

As organizations increasingly rely on artificial intelligence to enhance their employer branding efforts, the potential for bias in AI algorithms becomes a critical concern. Bias can manifest in various forms, from the data used to train models to the algorithms themselves, impacting recruitment outcomes and perpetuating existing inequalities. Understanding how bias arises and implementing strategies to mitigate its effects is essential for maintaining a fair, authentic, and inclusive employer brand.

Bias in AI algorithms often originates from the data upon which these systems are trained. If historical data reflects past hiring practices that favored certain demographics or profiles, the AI will likely replicate these preferences, unintentionally disadvantaging other candidates. For instance, if an organization has historically hired predominantly from specific universities or demographic groups, the AI may prioritize applications from similar backgrounds, thus perpetuating a cycle of homogeneity. This can lead to a lack of diversity within the workforce, which not only affects the employer's brand perception but also stymies innovation and creativity.

Furthermore, algorithmic bias can arise from the design of the AI system itself. If the developers do not consciously work towards eliminating bias, algorithms may incorporate flawed assumptions about candidate qualifications or characteristics. For instance, a recruitment tool that emphasizes certain keywords from resumes may inadvertently disadvantage candidates who use different terminology, even if their skills and experiences align closely with the job requirements. This highlights the importance of a thoughtful approach to algorithm design, emphasizing inclusivity and fairness alongside efficiency.

To combat these biases, organizations must take a proactive stance in their AI strategy. One effective approach is to diversify the datasets used in training AI models. This involves not only expanding the sources of data but also ensuring that the data represents a wide range of demographics, skill sets, and career paths. Organizations should strive for a balanced dataset that accurately reflects the rich diversity of the workforce they wish to build. Collaborating with external experts in data science and diversity can provide insights into best practices for creating and curating this data.

In addition to diversifying data sources, it is crucial to implement regular audits of AI algorithms to identify and rectify biases. These audits should evaluate the outcomes generated by the AI systems, focusing on how different demographic groups are represented in hiring decisions and subsequent employee performance metrics.

By systematically examining these outputs, organizations can identify discrepancies and take corrective action, such as adjusting the algorithms or refining the criteria used in candidate evaluations. This ongoing process fosters accountability and encourages continuous improvement in the AI systems employed.

Transparency is another key element in addressing bias in AI. Organizations should be open about how their AI systems operate, including the data sources, algorithms, and decision-making processes involved. Transparency builds trust not only with candidates but also among current employees who may be concerned about fairness and equity in their workplace. Communicating the steps taken to mitigate bias, such as the use of anonymized resumes during the initial screening process or the involvement of diverse hiring panels, reinforces the message that the organization is committed to fairness.

Moreover, fostering an inclusive workplace culture is essential for balancing the potential pitfalls of AI with its advantages. Organizations should create an environment where employees feel empowered to voice concerns about bias or discrimination they may encounter in AI-driven processes. Establishing channels for feedback, whether through anonymous surveys or open forums, encourages dialogue and allows organizations to address issues proactively and transparently. Training staff on recognizing and countering bias in AI systems further enhances this culture of inclusion, equipping them with the tools to navigate challenges effectively.

Education and training for HR professionals and hiring managers are paramount in ensuring that they understand the implications of AI in recruitment. This should encompass not only the technical aspects of how AI works but also the ethical considerations surrounding its use. Providing workshops or training sessions that address bias, diversity, and inclusion in AI can empower decision-makers to make informed choices when utilizing these tools. Such initiatives reinforce the organization's commitment to equity and demonstrate that AI is a tool for enhancing, rather than replacing, human judgment.

Another important consideration is the role of ethical guidelines in shaping the use of AI within employer branding. Organizations should establish clear ethical principles that guide their AI practices, ensuring that these align with their overall mission of promoting diversity and inclusion. By integrating ethical considerations into their AI strategies, companies can reinforce their commitment to fair hiring practices and establish a strong employer brand that resonates with a diverse talent pool.

Ultimately, addressing bias and fairness in AI algorithms is not just a technical challenge; it is a moral imperative that carries significant implications for employer branding. Organizations that prioritize fairness in their AI practices can enhance their reputation as inclusive employers, attracting a wider array of talent and fostering an environment where all employees feel valued and respected. This not only creates a more robust workforce but also positions the organization as a leader in ethical AI practices, further solidifying its brand in the competitive landscape.

The journey to eliminate bias from AI systems is ongoing and requires vigilance, commitment, and a willingness to adapt. As the landscape of employer branding continues to evolve, organizations must remain proactive in their efforts to ensure that their AI-driven processes reflect their values and commitment to diversity.By doing so, they can leverage the power of AI to build authentic, human-centric employer brands that resonate with candidates and employees alike, ultimately leading to a more equitable and inclusive workplace.

In the rapidly evolving landscape of employer branding, trust becomes a cornerstone of successful implementation of AI systems. As organizations leverage artificial intelligence to enhance their recruitment strategies, build candidate experiences, and strengthen their employer brands, the need to foster trust among potential and existing employees cannot be overstated. Trust is not merely a value; it's a critical component that influences perceptions, engagement, and ultimately, retention. In this context, organizations must be deliberate in their efforts to establish and maintain trust in AI systems.

At the outset, it is essential to recognize that trust in AI is multifaceted. It encompasses the transparency of algorithms, the ethical use of data, and the overall accountability of AI-powered systems. Each of these components contributes to a holistic understanding of how organizations can create a trustworthy AI framework that resonates with their workforce.

Transparency is perhaps the most significant factor in building trust in AI systems. Candidates and employees alike have a right to understand how AI influences their application processes, performance assessments, and career advancement opportunities. When organizations deploy AI tools for recruitment, they should provide clear communication about how these tools work. This includes explaining the data used, the criteria for decision-making, and the methodologies employed in predictive analytics. By demystifying the AI processes, organizations can alleviate concerns about bias, discrimination, or unfair treatment.

Furthermore, transparency extends beyond the technical workings of AI systems. Companies should cultivate an environment where feedback is not only welcomed but actively sought. Regularly engaging employees in discussions about their experiences with AI tools can foster a sense of inclusion and ownership over the processes that affect them. Surveys, focus groups, and open forums can serve as platforms for employees to voice their opinions and concerns, allowing organizations to adjust their AI implementations in response to feedback. This proactive approach not only builds trust but also enhances the effectiveness of AI tools by ensuring they align with employee expectations and needs.

The ethical use of data is another critical aspect of trust-building in AI systems. Organizations collecting data for AI-driven recruitment must adhere to stringent data protection standards and privacy regulations. This includes obtaining explicit consent from candidates regarding the use of their information and ensuring that data is stored securely. Transparency in data usage policies is vital; candidates should be informed about how their data will be utilized, who will have access to it, and how long it will be retained. By treating data responsibly and ethically, organizations can demonstrate their commitment to safeguarding employee privacy, thereby building trust in their AI systems.

Moreover, organizations must be vigilant in addressing potential biases that can arise in AI algorithms. AI systems are only as unbiased as the data fed into them. Historical data reflecting societal biases can inadvertently perpetuate discrimination in hiring processes. To combat this issue, organizations should conduct regular audits of their AI systems to identify and mitigate bias. This includes analyzing the outcomes of recruitment processes to ensure fairness and equity in decision-making. Engaging with third-party experts or utilizing bias detection tools can enhance the objectivity of these audits.

Training and educating staff about the implications of AI in recruitment processes is crucial for fostering a culture of trust. When employees understand AI's capabilities and limitations, they become better equipped to navigate its complexities. Organizations should invest in training sessions that cover the ethical dimensions of AI, emphasizing the importance of fairness, accountability, and transparency. By empowering employees with knowledge, organizations can cultivate a workforce that actively champions ethical AI practices and reinforces the trustworthiness of the systems in place.

Accountability is another pillar of trust in AI systems. Organizations must establish clear lines of accountability regarding AI decision-making. When a hiring decision is influenced by an AI tool, it is essential to have mechanisms in place to review and assess that decision. This includes having human oversight in the recruitment process where appropriate, allowing for human intervention when AI outputs raise concerns. By demonstrating that AI decisions are not made in isolation, organizations can reassure candidates and employees that their interests are being safeguarded.

Building trust in AI systems also requires organizations to embrace a mindset of continuous improvement. The technological landscape is dynamic, and AI tools will continue to evolve. Organizations should remain open to adapting their AI strategies based on new insights, technological advancements, and changing employee expectations. By communicating this commitment to ongoing improvement, organizations position themselves as responsible stewards of AI technology, fostering an environment where employees feel confident in the systems that influence their careers.

Finally, organizations can leverage storytelling as a tool for trust-building. Sharing success stories about how AI has positively impacted employees and recruitment outcomes can humanize the technology and underscore its value. Celebrating stories of diverse hires, improved candidate experiences, and enhanced employee engagement can reinforce the message that AI is a partner in achieving organizational goals rather than a faceless decision-maker. Such narratives can foster emotional connections with employees, enhancing their trust in the systems that support their career journeys.

In conclusion, building trust in AI systems within the realm of employer branding is an intricate yet vital endeavor. By prioritizing transparency, ethical data use, bias mitigation, accountability, continuous improvement, and effective storytelling, organizations can create a robust framework that nurtures trust. As AI continues to shape the future of recruitment and employee engagement, establishing trust will not only enhance the effectiveness of these systems but also solidify the organization's reputation as a responsible and forward-thinking employer. Ultimately, a foundation of trust in AI will empower organizations to attract, engage, and retain top talent while building a strong, authentic employer brand that resonates deeply with employees and candidates alike.

Leveraging AI for Global Employer Branding

In an increasingly interconnected world, organizations must recognize that their employer branding strategies cannot be one-size-fits-all. The cultural nuances, expectations, and values of potential employees can vary significantly across different regions and markets. As businesses expand globally, leveraging artificial intelligence (AI) to adapt employer branding strategies to diverse markets becomes not just advantageous but essential. This section explores how AI can facilitate the customization of employer branding efforts, ensuring that they resonate with local talent while maintaining the core identity of the organization.

To begin with, understanding the cultural context of each market is paramount. AI tools can analyze vast amounts of data from social media, job platforms, and online forums to identify the sentiments, preferences, and expectations of candidates in different regions. For instance, an AI-driven sentiment analysis tool can process conversations around employer brands in specific countries, revealing how local candidates perceive various employers. By tapping into this data, organizations can tailor their messaging and engagement strategies, making them more relevant and appealing to local talent pools.

One of the critical aspects of adapting employer branding strategies globally is language. AI-powered translation tools can assist in creating localized content that speaks directly to candidates in their native language. However, translation goes beyond mere linguistic conversion; it requires an understanding of local idioms, cultural references, and context. AI can facilitate this by employing natural language processing (NLP) algorithms that not only translate but also adapt the tone and style of the messaging to fit regional expectations. For example, a company may present its values and culture differently in a collectivist society compared to an individualistic one. Such nuanced communication can significantly enhance the effectiveness of employer branding campaigns.

Furthermore, AI can aid in identifying the most effective channels for reaching potential candidates in diverse markets. By analyzing data from various recruitment platforms and social media channels, AI algorithms can determine where different demographics spend their time and which platforms yield the highest engagement rates. For instance, while LinkedIn may be a dominant platform for professional networking in Western countries, younger candidates in some Asian markets may prefer platforms like TikTok or WeChat. By directing resources to the right platforms, organizations can maximize their reach and ensure that their employer branding efforts are not only noticed but also engaged with by the target audience.

AI can also help organizations develop targeted recruitment campaigns that align with local values and incentives. For example, in markets where work-life balance is highly valued, companies can emphasize their flexible working arrangements, wellness programs, and employee support initiatives in their branding. Conversely, in regions where career advancement is a primary motivator, organizations may choose to highlight their professional development programs, mentorship opportunities, and clear pathways for progression. By leveraging AI to analyze local job market trends and candidate preferences, companies can effectively position themselves as employers of choice in different regions.

In addition to attracting local talent, organizations must also consider how to engage and retain employees in diverse markets. AI can facilitate personalized onboarding experiences that cater to the cultural backgrounds of new hires. For instance, using AI-driven platforms, organizations can create tailored onboarding materials that resonate with the local culture and include relevant examples and case studies. This approach not only fosters a sense of belonging but also enhances the overall employee experience from the outset.

Continuing the theme of engagement, AI can also monitor employee sentiment and engagement levels in real-time through tools that analyze feedback from surveys, social media, and internal communication channels. These insights can help HR professionals identify potential issues or areas for improvement in real-time, allowing for timely interventions. In a global context, understanding how employees in different regions feel about their work environment can inform localized strategies to enhance engagement and retention.

Additionally, organizations should be aware of the ethical implications of their AI-driven employer branding strategies. As they adapt their approaches to suit diverse markets, it is essential to ensure that they are not inadvertently perpetuating biases or stereotypes. AI algorithms must be trained on diverse datasets that accurately reflect the populations being targeted. This approach mitigates the risk of cultural misrepresentation and ensures that the messaging resonates authentically with local audiences. Transparency in how AI tools are utilized and the data that informs them can also build trust among employees and candidates alike.

As companies increasingly rely on AI to shape their global employer branding strategies, they must remain agile and adaptable. The job market is dynamic, and shifts in cultural attitudes, economic conditions, and technological advancements can influence candidates' perceptions and expectations. Organizations should leverage AI analytics to continuously monitor trends and adjust their branding efforts accordingly. By establishing a feedback loop that incorporates real-time data, companies can respond swiftly to changes and maintain a strong, relevant employer brand across different markets.

Moreover, collaboration across global teams is essential to ensure that employer branding strategies are effectively aligned with the organization's overarching mission and values. AI can facilitate cross-functional collaboration by providing insights that inform decision-making at all levels.

For example, shared dashboards and reporting tools can allow HR teams worldwide to access data and insights, fostering a unified approach to employer branding while still respecting local differences.

In conclusion, adapting AI strategies for diverse markets is crucial for organizations seeking to build a strong global employer brand. By leveraging AI's capabilities in cultural analysis, language adaptation, targeted recruitment, and real-time engagement monitoring, companies can create localized branding initiatives that resonate with potential candidates and existing employees alike. As the workforce becomes increasingly global, those organizations that prioritize cultural sensitivity and leverage AI to tailor their employer branding efforts will not only attract top talent but also foster a diverse and engaged workforce that drives innovation and success.

In an increasingly globalized world, the ability to effectively adapt employer branding strategies to resonate with diverse cultural backgrounds is paramount. As organizations extend their reach beyond borders, understanding local customs, values, and expectations becomes a crucial component of the employer branding equation.

Leveraging artificial intelligence in this context offers a powerful avenue for tailoring messaging, engaging potential candidates, and ultimately cultivating a strong and authentic employer brand that transcends cultural barriers.

AI's capacity to analyze vast amounts of data allows organizations to gain insights into regional preferences, work cultures, and candidate behaviors. By utilizing AI algorithms, companies can dissect demographic information, social media trends, and economic indicators to craft employer branding messages that are not only relevant but also culturally sensitive. This data-driven approach ensures that branding efforts resonate with local talent pools while maintaining alignment with the organization's overarching values.

For instance, AI tools can analyze sentiment in job market conversations across different regions. By assessing social media posts, online forums, and industry reports, organizations can identify what potential candidates in specific geographies value most in an employer. In some cultures, work-life balance may be a significant draw, while in others, opportunities for career advancement or community engagement might take precedence. Understanding these nuances allows organizations to tailor their employer branding strategies, ensuring that messaging is not only attractive but also relevant to the local workforce.

Localization goes beyond mere translation of job postings and corporate communications; it involves a deeper understanding of cultural contexts and expectations. For example, while a playful and casual tone may resonate well with candidates in a creative industry in North America, the same approach could be perceived as unprofessional in more traditional markets such as Japan or Germany. AI can analyze existing job postings and candidate interactions to recommend adjustments in tone, language, and even imagery to better align with local cultural standards.

Moreover, AI-driven platforms can assist in creating localized candidate experiences. For instance, chatbots equipped with natural language processing capabilities can communicate with candidates in their native languages, providing personalized responses that reflect local dialects and expressions. This level of engagement not only enhances the candidate experience but also demonstrates a company's commitment to inclusivity and respect for diverse cultures. As candidates interact with these AI tools, their feedback can further inform adjustments and refinements to ensure the messaging remains effective and culturally appropriate.

In addition to enhancing recruitment efforts, AI can also play a pivotal role in promoting diversity and inclusion within global employer branding strategies. By analyzing hiring patterns and employee demographics, companies can identify gaps in representation and tailor their employer branding efforts to attract underrepresented groups in specific regions. For instance, AI can help organizations understand which demographics may feel marginalized or overlooked in their current branding strategies, prompting a reevaluation of marketing tactics and outreach initiatives.

Cultural sensitivity in employer branding also requires an awareness of local regulations and business practices. Different regions may have varying expectations regarding transparency, employee rights, and workplace norms. AI can facilitate compliance by analyzing legislative frameworks and suggesting branding approaches that align with local laws. For example, in some countries, publicizing employee testimonials may require adherence to privacy regulations. AI can provide insights on how to structure such content while respecting legal boundaries and cultural expectations.

A notable example of successful localization comes from a multinational technology company that expanded its operations in Southeast Asia. Initially, the company employed a one-size-fits-all approach to its employer branding, relying on its established corporate identity from Western markets. However, feedback from local candidates indicated a disconnect, with many feeling that the company's branding did not resonate with their cultural values. By leveraging AI analytics, the company gathered insights into local preferences and expectations. It then launched a targeted campaign that emphasized community involvement, work-life harmony, and respect for local traditions. The result was a significant increase in applications and improved perceptions of the employer brand within the region.

Social media platforms also offer valuable opportunities for localization. AI can analyze engagement metrics and content performance to determine which platforms are most popular in particular regions. For example, while LinkedIn may be the dominant professional network in North America and Europe, regions such as Asia-Pacific may favor platforms like WeChat or LINE for professional networking. Tailoring content to fit the preferred platforms ensures that employer branding initiatives reach the target audience effectively.

Furthermore, AI can assist organizations in identifying and connecting with local influencers who can amplify their employer brand. By analyzing social media connections, engagement levels, and content relevance, AI tools can identify key opinion leaders within specific markets. Partnering with these influencers can enhance the credibility of the employer brand, as potential candidates often seek validation from trusted voices within their communities.

As organizations navigate the complexities of global employer branding, the importance of ongoing evaluation and adjustment cannot be overstated. AI tools can facilitate continuous monitoring of brand perception and candidate engagement across diverse markets. Regularly analyzing feedback, sentiment, and engagement metrics allows organizations to remain agile, adapting their strategies in real time to meet the evolving expectations of local talent pools.

In summary, leveraging AI for cultural sensitivity and localization in employer branding is not merely an option but a necessity in today's global job market. By harnessing data-driven insights, adapting messaging, and fostering inclusive experiences, organizations can create authentic employer brands that resonate with diverse audiences. The ability to connect with candidates on a cultural level not only enhances recruitment efforts but also contributes to long-term employee engagement and retention. In a world where organizational success is increasingly tied to the strength of employer branding, embracing AI as a partner in this journey is essential for building a resilient and compelling brand that appeals to talent across the globe.

In the realm of global employer branding, organizations are increasingly recognizing the potential of artificial intelligence to drive engagement and attract diverse talent pools. Through the lens of AI, companies can tailor their approaches to different cultural contexts, leveraging technology to not only enhance their reach but also to resonate more deeply with local audiences. This section explores several case studies that exemplify best practices in leveraging AI for global employer branding.

One notable example comes from Unilever, a multinational consumer goods company that has effectively utilized AI-driven insights to refine its employer branding strategy across diverse markets. In an effort to attract young talent in various regions, Unilever implemented an AI-based recruitment platform that analyzes local labor market trends and candidate preferences. By employing predictive analytics, the company identified the traits that appeal most to potential hires in specific countries. For instance, in markets like India and Brazil, where millennials and Gen Z make up a significant percentage of the workforce, Unilever focused on highlighting its commitment to sustainability and social impact—values that resonate deeply with younger generations. This data-driven approach not only improved the quality of applications but also strengthened Unilever's reputation as an employer that genuinely understands and cares about the aspirations of its workforce.

Another compelling case study is that of IBM, which has harnessed AI to create a more inclusive and engaging employer brand on a global scale. The company adopted an AI-driven chatbot named "Watson Career Coach," designed to assist employees and potential candidates in navigating career opportunities within IBM. This tool, which is available in multiple languages, provides personalized career advice based on individual skills, market trends, and personal aspirations. By facilitating conversations and offering tailored recommendations, IBM has created a more engaging candidate experience that transcends geographical boundaries. The chatbot also collects data on user interactions, allowing IBM to continuously refine its employer branding messages to better align with local expectations and cultural nuances.

In Asia, the Japanese technology company Fujitsu has leveraged AI to enhance its employer branding efforts while emphasizing its commitment to diversity and inclusion.

Fujitsu implemented an AI analytics platform that assesses gender diversity within its workforce and identifies areas for improvement. This platform monitors hiring practices, employee retention rates, and promotions, providing actionable insights that enable the company to create targeted initiatives aimed at attracting female talent. By showcasing these efforts in its employer branding campaigns, Fujitsu has been able to position itself as a leader in promoting gender equality in a region where such initiatives are still emerging. This case illustrates how AI can be harnessed not only to bolster employer branding but also to drive meaningful change within organizations and their communities.

Additionally, a notable example from the tech industry is Google, which employs AI to optimize its global employer branding efforts through data-driven storytelling. Google utilizes machine learning algorithms to analyze employee feedback and social media sentiment across different markets. This data informs the creation of localized content that reflects the company's values while resonating with the unique cultural perspectives of diverse talent pools. For instance, in regions where work-life balance is a top priority, Google emphasizes its flexible work policies and employee well-being initiatives. By tailoring its messaging based on real-time data insights, Google has successfully built a global employer brand that feels authentic and relevant to candidates across the world.

Furthermore, Starbucks has implemented an AI-driven platform to enhance its recruitment strategy in various countries, focusing on the importance of cultural alignment in employer branding. The company recognized that its brand image and employee value proposition needed to resonate differently across different regions. Utilizing AI, Starbucks developed a localized recruitment campaign that not only highlighted the company's commitment to community engagement but also emphasized the unique aspects of its workplace culture that appeal to local candidates. By creating customized job descriptions and engaging in culturally relevant outreach, Starbucks has fostered a sense of belonging among its employees, which, in turn, strengthens its employer brand on a global scale.

In the financial services sector, HSBC has taken a proactive approach to global employer branding by leveraging AI in their talent acquisition process. The company employs AI tools for analyzing candidate data to identify top talent across various markets. By integrating AI-driven insights into their recruitment practices, HSBC has been able to streamline its processes and ensure a diverse pool of candidates. The organization has also utilized AI to enhance its employer branding on social media platforms, tailoring content to reflect the interests and values of audiences in specific countries. This targeted approach not only bolsters HSBC's brand image but also engages potential candidates in a more meaningful way.

These case studies collectively highlight several best practices for leveraging AI in global employer branding. A common thread among these organizations is their commitment to data-driven decision-making, which informs their branding strategies and enhances their understanding of local talent pools. Furthermore, the integration of AI tools into recruitment processes not only streamlines operations but also fosters a more engaging candidate experience. Each of these companies has demonstrated the importance of localizing employer branding efforts to resonate with diverse cultural contexts, showcasing the power of AI to create authentic and compelling narratives.

As businesses look to navigate the complexities of global employer branding, the lessons learned from these case studies provide a valuable roadmap. Organizations must remain agile, continuously adapting their strategies based on evolving market dynamics and candidate expectations. By implementing AI-driven tools and frameworks, companies can cultivate a strong, authentic employer brand that not only attracts top talent but also fosters a sense of belonging and engagement among employees worldwide. In doing so, they position themselves as leaders in the ever-competitive global talent landscape, ready to meet the challenges and opportunities of the future.

Measuring Success: AI Metrics and Analytics

In the rapidly evolving landscape of employer branding, where artificial intelligence (AI) plays an increasingly pivotal role, establishing effective Key Performance Indicators (KPIs) becomes essential for measuring success. KPIs provide measurable values that demonstrate how effectively a company is achieving its key business objectives. For organizations leveraging AI in their employer branding efforts, KPIs must be tailored to reflect the unique contributions of AI technologies while aligning with broader HR and business goals.

When defining KPIs for AI branding initiatives, it is vital to consider a blend of quantitative and qualitative metrics. Quantitative metrics provide hard data that can easily be analyzed, while qualitative metrics offer insights into employee sentiment and brand perception. The combination of these two types of indicators creates a well-rounded view of an organization's employer branding effectiveness.

One of the most significant KPIs for AI-driven employer branding is the time-to-hire. This metric not only reflects the efficiency of the recruitment process but also indicates how well AI tools are optimizing candidate sourcing and selection. For example, organizations utilizing AI-driven predictive analytics can identify the most suitable candidates faster by analyzing vast datasets and recognizing patterns in successful hires. A noticeable decrease in time-to-hire can signal that an organization is effectively using AI to streamline its recruitment process. Another crucial KPI is the quality of hire, which assesses the performance and retention of new employees over time. This metric can be gauged through performance reviews, employee satisfaction surveys, and retention rates. AI can play a significant role in enhancing the quality of hire by providing data-driven insights into candidate fit based on past performance and current job requirements. Organizations that track this metric can refine their AI algorithms and recruitment strategies, ensuring that they attract candidates who align closely with their company culture and values.

Candidate experience is another vital KPI, especially in the context of employer branding. AI tools can significantly improve candidate engagement through personalized communication, automated responses, and seamless application processes. Measuring candidate satisfaction through surveys and feedback forms can provide insights into how well the AI strategies are resonating with applicants. High candidate satisfaction correlates with a positive employer brand, which in turn can attract higher-quality talent.

Brand perception is a qualitative KPI that reflects how potential and current employees view the organization. This can be measured through social media sentiment analysis, employee reviews on platforms like Glassdoor, and online reputation assessments. AI tools can analyze vast amounts of social media data to gauge public sentiment about the brand, providing organizations with real-time insights into their employer branding efforts. A strong, positive brand perception is critical in attracting top talent and can be a strong differentiator in a competitive job market.

Engagement metrics within the organization, such as employee participation in surveys, training programs, and company events, can serve as another KPI for evaluating the effectiveness of AI in employer branding. High engagement levels often indicate a strong employer brand that resonates with employees. AI can facilitate engagement by offering personalized learning and development opportunities based on individual employee data, thereby fostering a culture of growth and satisfaction.

Retention rates are arguably one of the most important KPIs for assessing the long-term impact of employer branding strategies. Organizations that successfully leverage AI to create a supportive and engaging work environment can expect higher retention rates. Predictive analytics can help identify employees at risk of leaving by analyzing engagement levels, performance data, and external factors. By proactively addressing potential issues, organizations can enhance employee satisfaction and loyalty, ultimately strengthening their employer brand.

Another emerging KPI is the diversity of new hires. AI can play a crucial role in promoting diversity and inclusion in the hiring process by minimizing bias in candidate selection. Organizations should track the proportion of diverse candidates at various stages of the recruitment process, from applications to interviews to hires. A balanced approach to diversity not only enhances the employer brand but also promotes a culture of innovation and creativity within the organization.

The effectiveness of AI-driven recruitment marketing campaigns can also be measured through metrics such as click-through rates (CTR) on job advertisements, application completion rates, and social media engagement. These metrics provide insights into how well the organization is attracting candidates through its branding efforts. High CTR and application rates suggest that the messaging and targeting strategies are aligned with the audience's interests, reinforcing the organization's employer brand.

Finally, organizations should consider the cost-per-hire as a KPI for evaluating the financial efficiency of their AI branding initiatives. This metric encompasses the total cost associated with the recruitment process, including advertising, agency fees, and the time invested by HR personnel. By analyzing cost-per-hire in conjunction with other performance metrics, organizations can assess the return on investment (ROI) of their AI tools and strategies in employer branding.

In conclusion, the establishment of robust KPIs is crucial for organizations seeking to measure the success of their AI-driven employer branding initiatives. By focusing on a combination of quantitative and qualitative metrics—such as time-to-hire, quality of hire, candidate experience, brand perception, engagement levels, retention rates, diversity in hiring, recruitment marketing effectiveness, and cost-per-hire—HR professionals can gain valuable insights into their branding efforts. This data-driven approach enables organizations to refine their strategies continuously, ensuring they remain competitive and attractive to top talent in an ever-evolving job market. Ultimately, the effective measurement of success through well-defined KPIs empowers organizations to harness the full potential of AI in creating a strong, authentic employer brand that resonates with both potential and existing employees.

In the dynamic landscape of employer branding, the ability to adapt and refine strategies based on data-driven insights is paramount. With the advent of artificial intelligence, organizations can analyze recruitment data with unprecedented precision and depth. This analytical capability not only enhances the recruitment process but also contributes to a continuous improvement cycle that is essential for maintaining a competitive edge in attracting and retaining top talent.

At the heart of analyzing recruitment data is the concept of actionable insights. Organizations must move beyond merely collecting data; they need to interpret it in ways that inform decision-making. AI-powered analytics tools can sift through vast amounts of data from various sources—application tracking systems, candidate relationship management systems, social media, and employee feedback platforms. By leveraging machine learning algorithms, these tools can identify patterns and correlations that may not be immediately apparent. For instance, a company might find that candidates sourced from specific job boards tend to have higher retention rates than those from others. Such insights can guide recruitment strategies and resource allocation, ensuring that efforts are concentrated where they yield the best results.

Moreover, predictive analytics is a game-changer in understanding candidate behaviors and preferences. By analyzing historical data, AI can forecast future trends and behaviors. For example, if data shows that candidates with certain qualifications or backgrounds are more likely to accept job offers and remain with the company long-term, recruiters can adjust their sourcing strategies accordingly. This approach not only optimizes the recruitment funnel but also enhances the quality of hires, ultimately supporting the development of a strong employer brand.

Another vital aspect of recruitment data analysis is the evaluation of candidate experience. AI tools can analyze feedback collected through surveys and assessments to gauge the effectiveness of the recruitment process. Sentiment analysis, powered by natural language processing, can provide insights into candidates' perceptions of the application process, interview experiences, and overall engagement with the brand. By identifying pain points—such as lengthy application processes or poor communication—organizations can make targeted improvements that enhance the candidate experience. This is crucial, as a positive candidate experience can significantly bolster an employer's reputation and attract high-quality applicants.

Diversity and inclusion are also critical components of a strong employer brand. Analyzing recruitment data through the lens of diversity metrics enables organizations to assess the effectiveness of their inclusive hiring practices. AI tools can help identify any biases in the recruitment process, such as disparities in interview rates or offer acceptance among different demographic groups. By addressing these biases and refining recruitment strategies, organizations can create a more equitable hiring process that resonates with a broader audience. This not only strengthens the employer brand but also fosters a positive workplace culture that values diversity.

Furthermore, continuous improvement in recruitment practices requires a proactive approach to monitoring and evaluating the effectiveness of various recruitment channels. AI analytics can provide insights into which sourcing methods yield the highest-quality candidates and most successful hires. By regularly assessing conversion rates, time-to-fill metrics, and candidate satisfaction scores across different channels, organizations can pivot their strategies in real time. For instance, if data analytics reveal that a particular university partnership consistently produces high-performing interns, HR can deepen that relationship to create a talent pipeline.

To facilitate this ongoing analysis, organizations should adopt a flexible and responsive data management system. Integrating various data sources into a centralized platform allows for holistic analysis and reporting. Dashboards that visualize key performance indicators (KPIs) related to recruitment can offer real-time insights, enabling HR professionals to make informed decisions quickly. These visualizations can also help communicate the impact of recruitment strategies to stakeholders, fostering alignment and support for continuous improvement initiatives.

Moreover, the role of feedback loops in recruitment data analysis cannot be overstated. Incorporating feedback from new hires about their recruitment experience and their perception of the employer brand can provide invaluable insights. Using AI to analyze this feedback, organizations can identify trends and areas for enhancement. For example, if new hires consistently cite a lack of clarity in job descriptions as a concern, HR can refine job postings to ensure they accurately reflect the role and organizational culture. This iterative process reinforces the employer brand, ensuring that it remains authentic and appealing to prospective candidates.

As organizations engage in the cycle of data analysis and continuous improvement, it is essential to foster a culture of data-driven decision-making across all levels of the organization. Training HR professionals to interpret data insights and integrate them into recruitment strategies is vital.

This empowerment not only enhances the effectiveness of recruitment efforts but also demonstrates a commitment to innovation and excellence in employer branding.

Looking ahead, the integration of advanced AI technologies will further enhance the capabilities of data analysis in recruitment. Natural language processing will allow organizations to mine unstructured data from candidate communications, while advanced machine learning models will improve predictive analytics, refining the understanding of candidate behavior and preferences. By staying abreast of these technological advancements and continuously adapting their strategies, organizations can ensure their employer branding remains robust and relevant in a rapidly evolving job market.

In conclusion, analyzing recruitment data is not merely an operational task; it is a strategic imperative for organizations aiming to build a strong employer brand. By leveraging AI-powered analytics to gain actionable insights, organizations can optimize their recruitment practices, enhance candidate experiences, and foster diversity and inclusion. The commitment to continuous improvement, supported by a culture of data-driven decision-making, will enable organizations to attract and retain top talent, positioning them as employers of choice in the competitive talent landscape.

In today's data-driven landscape, the ability to effectively report and visualize metrics is essential for organizations leveraging AI in their employer branding efforts. The right tools and methodologies can transform raw data into actionable insights, making it easier for HR professionals and business leaders to assess the effectiveness of their strategies, identify areas for improvement, and communicate results to stakeholders. This section delves into the key aspects of reporting and visualization tools that can elevate employer branding initiatives powered by artificial intelligence.

First and foremost, organizations must understand the importance of selecting the right reporting tools that cater to their specific needs. Many businesses rely on traditional spreadsheet software for data analysis and reporting, but this approach often falls short when dealing with complex datasets generated by AI systems. Instead, organizations should consider adopting advanced business intelligence (BI) tools that provide enhanced capabilities for data visualization and reporting. Tools like Tableau, Power BI, and Google Data Studio allow users to create interactive dashboards, graphs, and charts that can simplify the interpretation of metrics related to recruitment, employee engagement, and brand perception.

One of the standout features of modern BI tools is their ability to integrate with multiple data sources. For organizations employing AI-driven recruitment strategies, this is particularly beneficial as it allows for the aggregation of data from various platforms—such as Applicant Tracking Systems (ATS), Human Resource Information Systems (HRIS), and social media channels. By consolidating this information, HR professionals can generate comprehensive reports that provide a holistic view of their employer branding performance, ultimately leading to more informed decision-making.

Visualization is not just about creating appealing graphics; it's about telling a story that resonates with stakeholders. An effective visualization should not only present data but also highlight trends, correlations, and anomalies. For instance, if an organization implements an AI-driven recruitment campaign, visualizing the data can reveal insights into how different demographics respond to job postings, the efficiency of various recruitment channels, and the overall candidate journey. By displaying this information in a clear, digestible format, organizations can easily communicate the impact of their AI strategies to executives, team members, and other stakeholders, fostering a culture of transparency and data-driven decision-making.

When designing reports, HR professionals should consider the audience and tailor their visuals accordingly. For example, executives may prefer high-level summaries that focus on key performance indicators (KPIs) and strategic outcomes, while recruitment teams might benefit from more detailed analyses that explore the nuances of candidate behavior throughout the hiring process. Utilizing a combination of summary reports and detailed dashboards can ensure that all stakeholders receive the information they need, in the format they prefer.

Another critical aspect of effective reporting is the integration of predictive analytics into the visualization process. With AI's capability to analyze historical data and forecast future trends, organizations can create dynamic reports that not only reflect past performance but also project future outcomes. For example, if an organization identifies a trend of declining candidate engagement in a particular recruitment channel, predictive analytics can help forecast how this trend may evolve, enabling proactive adjustments to their strategies. By incorporating predictive elements into their reporting, organizations can pivot swiftly and strategically, ensuring that their employer branding remains competitive and compelling.

Furthermore, organizations should emphasize the importance of real-time reporting. In the fast-paced world of talent acquisition, timely insights are invaluable. The ability to track and visualize metrics in real-time allows HR teams to respond quickly to emerging trends and challenges. For instance, if a sudden spike in applications for a specific role occurs, teams can utilize real-time analytics to assess the effectiveness of their AI-driven marketing efforts and make necessary adjustments on the fly. This agility can be a significant advantage in a competitive job market where top talent is often in high demand.

To enhance the effectiveness of reporting and visualization tools, organizations must also prioritize data literacy among their HR teams. While advanced tools provide powerful functionalities, they are only as effective as the individuals using them. Training sessions on data analysis and visualization techniques can empower HR professionals to extract meaningful insights from their datasets confidently. By cultivating a culture of data literacy, organizations can ensure that their teams are equipped to leverage the full potential of AI in their employer branding efforts.

In addition to internal reporting, organizations should also consider how they communicate their employer brand externally. Data visualization can play a critical role in marketing and public relations efforts, showcasing an organization's commitment to diversity, employee satisfaction, and innovative practices. For example, an organization might create infographics that highlight key metrics related to employee engagement or diversity hiring initiatives. These visuals can be shared on social media, incorporated into recruitment materials, or presented at industry events, helping to craft a compelling narrative that resonates with prospective candidates.

Finally, organizations should regularly evaluate and iterate on their reporting and visualization processes. The landscape of employer branding and AI is rapidly evolving, and staying ahead of the curve requires ongoing adjustment and refinement of strategies. By soliciting feedback from stakeholders and analyzing the effectiveness of existing reports and visuals, organizations can identify gaps and opportunities for improvement.

Continuous improvement not only enhances the overall reporting process but also reinforces the commitment to building a strong, authentic employer brand that resonates with both potential and existing employees.

In conclusion, effective reporting and visualization tools are integral to measuring success in AI-driven employer branding efforts. By selecting the right tools, tailoring reports to specific audiences, integrating predictive analytics, fostering data literacy, and continuously refining processes, organizations can unlock the full potential of their data. This not only enhances their ability to attract and retain top talent but also strengthens their overall employer brand, ensuring they remain competitive in an ever-evolving job market. Through a strategic approach to reporting and visualization, organizations can create a compelling narrative that aligns with their employer branding goals, ultimately resonating with candidates and employees alike.

The Future of Employer Branding with AI

As we move further into the digital age, the landscape of employer branding is being reshaped by an array of emerging AI technologies and trends that hold the potential to redefine how organizations attract, engage, and retain talent. The rapid advancement of AI is providing innovative solutions to longstanding challenges within human resources, paving the way for more effective, efficient, and personalized employer branding strategies. Understanding these trends is crucial for organizations aiming to stay at the forefront of talent acquisition and retention.

One of the most significant trends shaping the future of employer branding is the rise of conversational AI. Tools such as chatbots and virtual assistants are becoming increasingly sophisticated, enabling organizations to engage with potential candidates in real-time. These AI-driven solutions can answer queries, provide information about job roles, and even guide candidates through the application process. By offering immediate responses and personalized interactions, conversational AI enhances the candidate experience, making it more likely that top talent will continue to engage with the employer's brand.

Moreover, conversational AI can be programmed to reflect an organization's brand voice and values, creating a cohesive and authentic experience for candidates. For instance, a company that prides itself on its innovative culture might utilize a chatbot that engages in playful conversation, reflecting that ethos. This level of personalization not only helps in attracting candidates who resonate with the brand but also sets the tone for what they can expect as employees.

Another emerging trend is the use of AI in enhancing employer branding through video content. Video marketing has long been recognized as a powerful tool for storytelling, and AI is now facilitating the creation and distribution of this content. AI algorithms can analyze data to identify the types of videos that resonate most with the target audience, enabling companies to tailor their messaging effectively. Furthermore, AI-powered video editing tools can automate the production process, allowing organizations to create high-quality content quickly and cost-effectively.

The incorporation of augmented reality (AR) and virtual reality (VR) technologies into employer branding strategies is also on the rise. These technologies provide immersive experiences that can showcase company culture, office environments, and employee testimonials in a way that traditional methods cannot. For example, a company might offer virtual tours of its workplace or simulate a day in the life of an employee through VR experiences. Such innovative approaches not only attract candidates but also provide them with a realistic view of what to expect, thus improving the likelihood of hiring the right fit for the organization.

As organizations strive to build authentic employer brands, the role of data analytics cannot be overstated. Advanced analytics powered by AI can provide deep insights into employee sentiment and engagement levels. By analyzing vast amounts of data collected from employee surveys, social media, and online reviews, organizations can gain a clear understanding of their brand perception in the job market. This data-driven approach enables HR professionals to identify areas for improvement and align their employer branding strategies with the expectations and desires of current and potential employees.

Furthermore, predictive analytics is emerging as a game-changer in anticipating talent needs and workforce dynamics. By leveraging historical data and AI algorithms, organizations can forecast future hiring trends, skill gaps, and employee turnover rates. This foresight allows companies to proactively refine their employer branding strategies, ensuring they remain appealing to top talent. For instance, if predictive analytics indicate an upcoming skills gap in a specific area, organizations can adjust their branding efforts to highlight development opportunities, training programs, and career growth to attract candidates with those skills.

The integration of AI in employee development and training is another trend that is set to reshape employer branding. AI-driven learning platforms can provide personalized training experiences tailored to individual employee needs and career aspirations. By promoting a culture of continuous learning and development, organizations can position themselves as desirable employers that invest in their workforce. This emphasis on growth and development not only enhances employee satisfaction and retention but also contributes positively to the overall employer brand.

As AI technologies continue to evolve, ethical considerations surrounding their use are becoming increasingly prominent. Organizations must navigate the complexities of data privacy, algorithmic bias, and transparency in AI systems. Building a responsible AI framework that prioritizes ethical practices is essential for maintaining trust with candidates and employees alike. Companies that demonstrate a commitment to ethical AI use will position themselves as leaders in the employer branding space, attracting talent that values corporate responsibility.

The future of employer branding is also closely tied to the concept of employee advocacy. With the rise of social media and online platforms, employees have become powerful brand ambassadors. AI can facilitate the identification and engagement of these advocates, enabling organizations to harness their influence effectively. By leveraging AI tools to monitor employee sentiment and online activity, companies can create strategies that empower employees to share their positive experiences, thereby amplifying the employer brand organically.

Finally, companies must be prepared to adapt to the global nature of the workforce. As remote work becomes more prevalent, the need for localized employer branding strategies will be paramount. AI can assist organizations in understanding cultural nuances and preferences across different regions, allowing for more effective recruitment campaigns. By tailoring their branding efforts to resonate with diverse audiences, companies can enhance their appeal on a global scale, attracting top talent from various backgrounds.

In summary, the convergence of emerging AI technologies and trends is set to revolutionize the future of employer branding. Opportunities abound for organizations willing to embrace these innovations, from enhancing candidate experiences through conversational AI and immersive technologies to leveraging data analytics for informed decision-making. As the job market continues to evolve, staying ahead of these trends will be crucial for organizations seeking to create strong, authentic employer brands that resonate with both current and potential employees. By harnessing the power of AI thoughtfully and ethically, businesses can not only navigate the complexities of the modern talent landscape but also build lasting connections with top talent.

The rapid evolution of artificial intelligence is reshaping the landscape of employer branding, creating new challenges and opportunities for organizations aiming to attract and retain top talent. As we look towards the future workforce, it is essential for businesses to adopt a forward-thinking approach that harnesses AI's capabilities to address the changing needs and expectations of employees. Preparing for this future involves a multi-faceted strategy that emphasizes adaptability, inclusivity, and a deep understanding of emerging trends in both technology and workplace culture.

One of the most significant shifts in the workforce is the increasing demand for flexibility and remote work options. With the rise of digital nomadism and a growing number of employees desiring a better work-life balance, organizations must leverage AI to create tailored experiences that resonate with diverse employee needs. AI-driven analytics can provide insights into employee preferences, enabling HR leaders to design work environments that support hybrid models, flexible hours, and personalized benefits packages. By actively listening to employee feedback and utilizing AI tools to analyze this data, companies can cultivate a more agile employer brand that adapts to the evolving expectations of the future workforce.

Moreover, the future workforce will likely prioritize values such as sustainability, diversity, and social responsibility. As a result, organizations must not only define their employer value proposition but also demonstrate their commitment to these values through actionable strategies.

AI can play a pivotal role in this journey by enabling companies to track their progress on diversity and inclusion initiatives, measure employee engagement, and gauge the effectiveness of corporate social responsibility (CSR) efforts. Through sentiment analysis and data visualization tools, organizations can communicate their values authentically, allowing potential and existing employees to connect with the brand on a deeper level.

In addition to external branding, companies must also focus on internal culture. The future workforce will be composed of individuals who seek more than just a paycheck; they will crave meaningful work, opportunities for professional growth, and a sense of belonging. AI can facilitate a more personalized employee experience by identifying skills gaps, recommending tailored learning and development programs, and fostering mentorship opportunities. By employing machine learning algorithms to analyze employee performance data, organizations can create individualized career pathways that empower employees to achieve their professional goals while aligning with the company's objectives.

Furthermore, as businesses become more globalized, cultural sensitivity will be paramount in preparing for the future workforce. AI can assist in this regard by providing insights into the cultural nuances of different markets, helping companies adapt their employer branding strategies accordingly. For instance, AI-driven tools can analyze social media trends and engagement metrics across various regions, enabling organizations to tailor their messaging to resonate with local audiences. This localized approach not only enhances brand perception but also demonstrates a company's commitment to understanding and valuing diverse cultures.

Training and development will also be transformed by AI as organizations seek to remain competitive in an ever-evolving job market. Advanced AI technologies, including natural language processing and machine learning, can create adaptive learning platforms that respond to individual employee needs. These platforms can assess an employee's current skill set, identify areas for improvement, and curate personalized learning pathways that leverage both internal resources and external courses. By fostering a culture of continuous learning and leveraging AI to facilitate professional development, organizations can position themselves as attractive employers that invest in their workforce's growth.

As we consider the future, it is essential to recognize that the role of AI in employer branding extends beyond mere automation. While AI tools can streamline processes and enhance efficiency, they must also be integrated into a broader strategy that prioritizes human connection. The future workforce will expect organizations to leverage technology to enhance the employee experience, not replace it. Therefore, businesses must strive to create a human-centric workplace where AI serves as an enabler of collaboration, creativity, and innovation.

To prepare for the future workforce, companies must also embrace the ethical considerations surrounding AI. As organizations increasingly rely on AI to drive decision-making, they must ensure that their systems are transparent, fair, and free from bias. This commitment to ethical AI practices not only builds trust with employees but also enhances the overall employer brand. Organizations that prioritize ethics in their AI initiatives will likely attract top talent who value integrity and social responsibility.

Another critical component in preparing for the future workforce is fostering a culture of agility and resilience. The ability to pivot quickly in response to changing market dynamics will be paramount for organizations that wish to thrive in the future. AI can support this agility by providing real-time insights into workforce trends, enabling companies to anticipate challenges and proactively address them. By harnessing predictive analytics, organizations can make informed decisions about talent acquisition, engagement, and retention strategies, ensuring they remain competitive in a rapidly shifting environment.

Ultimately, preparing for the future workforce requires a holistic approach that integrates AI into every aspect of employer branding. By leveraging AI tools and strategies, organizations can create a stronger, more authentic employer brand that resonates with potential and existing employees. The future workforce will demand flexibility, inclusivity, and a commitment to values, and companies that embrace these principles will be well-positioned to attract and retain top talent.

As we move forward, the question is not simply how organizations can leverage AI for employer branding, but rather how they can integrate AI into a broader strategy that prioritizes the human experience. In doing so, businesses will unlock the potential of their workforce, empowering employees to thrive in a dynamic and increasingly complex world. The journey toward a future-driven employer brand is one of continuous learning, adaptation, and commitment to creating an environment where both AI and human talent can flourish together.

In a world that is increasingly driven by technological advancements, sustaining innovation in employer branding has become paramount for organizations seeking to attract and retain top talent. As artificial intelligence (AI) continues to evolve, it offers unprecedented opportunities for companies to enhance their employer brands, but leveraging these tools effectively requires a forward-thinking approach. The key to sustaining innovation lies in the ability to blend technology with human insight, fostering a culture that not only embraces change but thrives on it.

To maintain a competitive edge in the talent marketplace, organizations must adopt an agile mindset. This involves regularly assessing and iterating on employer branding strategies to ensure they resonate with the ever-changing expectations of potential and current employees. AI can play an instrumental role in this process by providing real-time data analytics, enabling organizations to gauge sentiment, engagement levels, and overall brand perception. By continuously monitoring these indicators, HR professionals can identify trends and adjust their strategies proactively, rather than reactively.

Furthermore, it is essential to cultivate a holistic approach to employer branding that integrates AI with authentic storytelling and genuine employee experiences. This goes beyond just using AI to create slick marketing campaigns; it requires a commitment to transparency and authenticity in how brands present themselves. Companies that leverage AI tools to gather employee feedback and insights can craft compelling narratives that reflect the true culture and ethos of the organization. Sharing these stories not only helps to attract potential employees but also reinforces the commitment to existing staff, fostering a sense of pride and loyalty.

Another vital aspect of sustaining innovation in employer branding is recognizing the importance of personalization. Modern job seekers value experiences that feel tailored to their unique skills and aspirations. AI-powered tools enable organizations to segment their audience and deliver targeted messaging that speaks directly to the needs and desires of potential candidates. By utilizing machine learning algorithms to analyze candidate profiles, organizations can create personalized job recommendations, career development opportunities, and onboarding experiences that resonate on an individual level. This tailored approach not only enhances the candidate experience but also reinforces the employer brand as one that genuinely cares about its employees' futures.

Moreover, sustaining innovation requires an ongoing commitment to diversity and inclusion in employer branding efforts. AI can facilitate more equitable hiring processes by minimizing biases and ensuring that a wider array of candidates are considered. Organizations must actively seek out diverse talent and utilize AI-driven analytics to evaluate the effectiveness of their diversity initiatives. By fostering an inclusive culture that values diverse perspectives, companies can not only enhance their employer brand but also drive innovation from within. A diverse workforce is proven to yield greater creativity and problem-solving capabilities, ultimately benefiting the organization as a whole.

Investing in employee development and well-being is another cornerstone of sustained innovation. Companies that prioritize continuous learning and growth opportunities will not only attract top talent but also retain it. AI can support these initiatives by analyzing skills gaps within the organization and recommending personalized training programs. This dynamic approach to employee development not only enhances the employer brand but also positions the organization as a leader in fostering a culture of growth and innovation.

In addition to internal strategies, organizations must also be vigilant in monitoring their external brand perception.

Social media and online reviews play a critical role in how potential candidates perceive an employer. AI can assist in sentiment analysis, allowing organizations to track and respond to feedback in real-time. By actively engaging with employees and candidates on various platforms, organizations can demonstrate their commitment to addressing concerns and continuously improving their brand. This engagement not only enhances the employer brand but also builds trust and credibility in the eyes of potential hires.

The future of employer branding will also necessitate collaboration across departments. HR, marketing, and IT must work together to create cohesive strategies that leverage AI's capabilities effectively. Cross-functional teams can bring diverse perspectives to the table, ensuring that employer branding initiatives are aligned with the overall business goals and resonate with both employees and external candidates. This collaborative approach fosters innovation and allows for the rapid testing and iteration of new ideas, driving the organization forward in a competitive landscape.

Finally, sustaining innovation in employer branding requires a commitment to ethical AI practices. As organizations leverage AI technologies, they must remain vigilant about data privacy, algorithmic bias, and transparency. Building trust with employees and candidates is paramount; therefore, organizations should prioritize ethical considerations in their AI strategies. By being transparent about how AI is used in recruitment and branding efforts, companies can foster a sense of security and trust among their workforce.

In conclusion, sustaining innovation in employer branding in the age of AI requires a multifaceted approach that embraces agility, authenticity, personalization, diversity, and ethical considerations. Organizations that effectively harness the power of AI while maintaining a human-centric focus will not only attract top talent but will also foster a culture of loyalty and engagement among existing employees. The key lies in continuously evolving strategies, leveraging data-driven insights, and cultivating an inclusive environment that values growth and innovation. By doing so, companies can establish themselves as leaders in the talent marketplace, creating a strong, authentic employer brand that resonates deeply with individuals in a rapidly changing world.

About Patrice Espiche

Patrice Espiche has been active in the field of Employer Branding, HR, and Talent Acquisition in the DACH region for many years. He has successfully implemented numerous projects and has been deeply engaged with the benefits, opportunities, and risks of AI in this field since the introduction of ChatGPT.

With experience in responsible positions across startups and large corporations, he brings extensive knowledge in Employer Branding, HR, and Talent Acquisition. Through hands-on project execution, he is an early adopter who integrates innovative approaches aligned with current trends.

Patrice Espiche has a background in psychology and is driven by the mission of creating a positive and engaging work environment. He believes in leveraging progress and staying open to new developments as key factors for generating the most value for companies and employees alike.